LONDON
in your pocket

MICHELIN
Travel Publications

KU-093-207

MAIN CONTRIBUTOR: CHRISTOPHER PICK

PHOTOGRAPH CREDITS
Photos supplied by The Travel Library, unless
otherwise stated: 107; A Amsel 79, 122; Lee Frost
title page, 15, 17, 18, 20; Ian Hunt 88; Roger
Howard front cover, 13, 19, 21, 25, 28, 29, 30, 31,
32, 33, 34, 37, 39, 41, 43, 44, 51, 52 (bottom), 55,
57, 59, 62, 65, 66, 68, 72, 73, 77, 78, 83, 97, 101,
105, 112, 121, 125, 126; David McGill 52 (top);
Rob Moore 5, 8, 26, 42, 45, 47, 49, 53, 54, 63, 75,
82, 87, 92, 116; R Richardson 22, 46, 69, 71, 80,
84, 85, 91, 95; Peter Terry 23; Andy Williams back
cover, 7, 35, 61, 64, 70, 96.
Other photos: Daily Mail 11.

*Front cover: members of the guards band; back cover: Tower
Bridge at night; title page: Horseguard*

MANUFACTURE FRANÇAISE DES PNEUMATIQUES MICHELIN

Place des Carmes-Déchaux – 63000 Clermont-Ferrand (France)

© Michelin et Cie. Propriétaires-Éditeurs 1997

Dépôt légal Avril 97 – ISBN 2-06-651101-3 – ISSN 1272-1689

No part of this publication may be reproduced in any form

without the prior permission of the publisher.

Printed in Spain 04-00/4

MICHELIN TRAVEL PUBLICATIONS
Michelin Tyre plc
The Edward Hyde Building
38 Clarendon Road
WATFORD Herts WD1 1SX - UK
☎ (01923) 415000
www.michelin-travel.com

MICHELIN TRAVEL PUBLICATIONS
Michelin North America
One Parkway South
GREENVILLE, SC 29615
☎ 1-800 423-0485
www.michelin-travel.com

CONTENTS

INTRODUCTION

'When a man is tired of London, he is tired
of life; for there is in London all that life can
afford.' So spoke in 1777 Dr Samuel
Johnson, the celebrated essayist and giant of
London literary life. His words ring as true
today as they did more than 200 years ago,
for London can fairly claim to be one of the
world's greatest capitals: exciting and lively,
large yet highly accessible, and very much a
human city.

The key to getting the most out of
London is to appreciate the continual
intermingling of past and present. In
contrast with many other cities, London has
never been subjected to grand master
development plans – the city has instead
evolved through constant but gradual
change. Each generation did, of course,
build anew and impose its own stamp on the
city – a process that continues still. London
lost many of its historic sites during the
Second World War, and some of the
buildings that replaced them were sadly
lacking in imagination. Many of these,
however, are now being replaced with more
pleasing ones.

As it did in Dr Johnson's day, London
'affords' every facet of a contemporary city:
countless clubs and nightspots, shops of all
kinds, from mega-stores to boutiques selling
the latest fashions and art and craftwork,
entertainments and exhibitions to suit every
interest. But all this happens in streets and
quarters that are full of links with past
Londoners, and mostly remain on a human
scale.

The best way of getting to know London is
to explore the city on foot. The six walks in
this guide are designed to provide helpful

introductions to some of the most interesting areas to explore. Strike off on your own whenever you want to – you will soon discover that London surely remains, to quote a writer three centuries earlier than Dr Johnson, 'the flower of cities all'.

The fountains of Trafalgar Square, with the church of St Martin-in-the-Fields behind.

GEOGRAPHY

London's history is inexorably linked to the Thames. The city was founded at the easiest downstream crossing-point, shortly before the river widens as it flows eastwards towards the sea. From the earliest days, travellers from the Continent would land at Dover and then follow the ancient routes through Kent to London. Meanwhile, vessels transporting men and goods sailed up the Thames to berth there. Importing and exporting, at first via the wharves on the river's north and south banks, then through the purpose-built 19C docks, became a central part of London's economy. Only in the last quarter century or so has the city lost its docks, as new container berths with easier transport access have been constructed further downstream.

Some miles north and south of the city centre, two ranges of gentle hills, now mostly covered with suburban development, also help to define London. The city lies in a shallow bowl, which in summer retains heat.

HISTORY

The Romans

London was founded shortly after the **Roman** invasion of Britain in AD 43 and expanded rapidly, becoming an important trading and cultural centre, the capital of Roman Britain and the hub of the Romans' road system. By around AD 200 **Londinium**, prosperous and sophisticated, boasted a forum, amphitheatre, temple and basilica. A wooden bridge crossed the Thames near the site of London Bridge. Wharves served the flourishing overseas trade, and walls encircled the city; their line was to mark

London's landward boundary for more than 1 000 years.

Under Roman domination, London became a world city – a focus of commercial, political and cultural power, a major international port, and a large population centre – and it remains so today.

The City of London

Although trade continued during the **Saxon** period, London declined in importance. Its revival began in the 9C, and by the time of the **Norman** invasion it was once again a prosperous, powerful and independent-

The foundation stones of the Roman Temple of Mithras can be seen in Queen Victoria Street.

A map of London showing a view of the city in the late 18C.

minded city. Indeed, so much so that after his conquest, **William I** thought it necessary to build the White Tower (the main keep of the Tower of London), on the eastern edge of the City, to remind its citizens of his might.

William distanced himself from London and its rebellious people by building his principal palace at Westminster, a few miles upstream. The tension which built up during this period between the court and the government and administration in Westminster, and trade bodies based in the City of London, still exists today.

The City of London received its independence from the monarchy and Westminster through a series of royal charters. The City's wealthy burghers have always paid taxes, and have lent money to the Crown, but it has remained self-governing over the centuries, through the

Corporation of London. Bodies known as guilds were also formed to protect and further the interests of the many different traders – apothecaries, tailors, goldsmiths and so on – who operated in the City. London was already a cosmopolitan place. Credit was provided to merchants and to the Crown by Jews and, after their expulsion in 1290, by the Milanese.

The Golden Age

The 16C and 17C saw the City's Golden Age. Merchants and speculators grew rich from financing the voyages of the Elizabethan explorers, who established trading posts around the world. Trade and manufacturing expanded. So too did the population, which had increased from around 40 000 in the 14C and 15C to 200 000 (the same as that of Roman London) by the turn of the 17C.

Although the City remained London's principal residential and commercial area, expansion was slowly taking place. Areas such as Smithfield and Holborn, immediately outside the City walls, were developed as the cost of land within the City became exhorbitant. Noblemen built grand houses along the Strand (the main route to Westminster), and further upstream in Chelsea and towards Richmond and Hampton Court.

Ironically, two major disasters, the **Great Plague** and the **Great Fire**, stimulated the expansion of London. Some 100 000 people died in the plague epidemic of 1664-65, and a year later the Great Fire destroyed the heart of the City. Many of those who fled, from pestilence and fire, never returned, settling in the new suburbs. Although trade soon resumed, and the City itself was rebuilt within a generation, it began to decline as a centre of population.

The New London

As London expanded between the 1660s and the 1830s, some of the city's most handsome squares and houses were built. In Covent Garden, Soho and Bloomsbury the nobility and prosperous merchants moved into elegant residences. The areas patronized by fashionable society were St James's, Mayfair and Piccadilly, with their shops, theatres and coffee houses. In close proximity lived London's poor, often in appalling conditions of poverty and ill health.

By 1800 London was the world's largest city, with a population of around 1 million, and an increasingly important manufacturing centre. The 'dark Satanic mills' of William Blake's poetic vision were not in the industrial north of England, but on London's South Bank, near where he lived. The 19C brought London's greatest period of expansion, and also, for the first time, a division between where people worked and lived. The development of public transport – horse-drawn omnibuses and trams, overground railways, then the underground system – enabled people to commute from the suburbs to work.

Modern London

By 1911, inner London's population had grown to 6.5 million. The city expanded rapidly, flooding out into the countryside in all directions, engulfing villages and small towns that had previously been quite separate rural communities. To this day, these places, such as Hampstead and

St Paul's stands triumphant during the Blitz.

Camden Town, have managed to retain distinct identities, and still contribute to London's diversity.

During the 19C and early 20C, London was the hub of the British Empire, and many imposing government and commercial buildings date from this period. Although the West End did not suffer to such an extent, the City and the East End were badly damaged during the **Second World War** in the aerial bombardment known as the London Blitz. Constructions of the 1950s and 1960s were of variable quality. Since then, there has been substantial piecemeal development throughout London, especially in the City, while the old Docklands area is being developed into a new business and residential district.

THE PEOPLE AND CULTURE

Variety and cosmopolitanism are London's greatest assets. Even in central London, widely differing areas, with contrasting characteristics and histories, lie cheek by jowl as buildings from more than three centuries jostle for space.

London's cosmopolitanism derives from its willingness, over many centuries, to embrace and adopt newcomers. There are, of course, many Londoners whose families have belonged to the capital for generations, but the city's enormous population explosions, in the 16C and 17C, and again in the 19C and 20C, brought countless people into the city.

Most came to find work. Since the 12C, London has been England's (and, later, Britain's) premier city. As such, it was the centre of court and government, of administration, and of trade and finance; all these functions demanded a huge workforce, and continue to do so.

Indeed, the life of the capital itself – its transport, shops, restaurants, schools and all the myriad services upon which Londoners and visitors alike depend – provides a multitude of jobs.

Over the centuries people have come from the English countryside, Scotland, Wales and Ireland, especially when those countries were experiencing poverty and starvation. They came from Europe, among them Huguenots from France in the late 17C, Jews from eastern Europe and Russia in the late 19C, and refugees from Nazi terror in the 1930s.

During the Second World War, London became home to people from all parts of

Over 2000 years the old city has endlessly revitalised itself by embracing immigrants, most recently Huguenots, Jews and Asians. Go to the Sunday morning market in the East End's Petticoat Lane and afterwards lunch in a Bengali restaurant in Brick Lane (once the haunt of Jack the Ripper).

Europe. Since then, partly as a consequence of Britain's past imperial might, people have arrived from Asia, Africa, the Caribbean and the Far East.

All these people, whether they are first-generation or multi-generation Londoners, contribute to the city's cosmopolitan flavour. Their personal, social, religious and cultural experiences enrich the city, and in turn they absorb some of the essence of the city and become Londoners themselves.

The pigeons in Trafalgar Square can be very persistent.

MUST SEE

Westminster★★★
The **Palace of Westminster★★★**, seat of both
Houses of Parliament, and **Westminster
Abbey★★★**, where coronations and royal
weddings are held, will be the starting point
for many visitors' exploration of London.

The City★★★
Also known as the Square Mile, with its
network of narrow streets and contrasting
modern buildings housing London's
financial and business sector, the City forms
the financial heart of London, at its liveliest
at lunchtime. It contains St Paul's Cathedral,
the **Temple★★**, many churches and the
Museum of London★★.

St Paul's Cathedral★★★
Christopher Wren's Baroque masterpiece,
built between 1675 and 1708 following the
Great Fire of London.

Tower of London★★★
The capital's most awesome building is a
900-year-old repository of history built as a
fortress, prison and place of execution. It
houses the Crown Jewels.

British Museum★★★
A vast and stunning collection of artefacts
from all the great civilizations of the world,
including the Rosetta Stone and the Elgin
Marbles.

National Gallery★★★
Over 2 000 paintings from throughout
Europe, spanning the 13C to the end of the
19C.

Tate Gallery★★★
Renamed **Tate Britain** after the **Tate Modern** opened in Bankside, this contains the national collection of post-1600 British art.

South Kensington Museums★★★
The **Natural History Museum★★**, **Science Museum★★★** and the **Victoria and Albert Museum★★★**, featuring decorative arts, are close to each other, but you will need more than one visit to take in all their treasures.

The triumphant statue of Richard Lionheart stands proudly outside the Neo-Gothic Palace of Westminster.

Regent's Park★★★
A tour of the park should include Nash's famous terraces which surround much of the park. Inside the park are **London Zoo★★** to the north, Queen Mary's Gardens and the Open-Air Theatre.

Greenwich★★★
Combine a river trip on the Thames with a visit to the **Royal Naval College★★**, **National Maritime Museum★★** and the Cutty Sark, or maybe you will prefer to spend the day in the **Millennium Dome**.

Hampton Court Palace★★★
The magnificent Tudor palace of Henry VIII, with fine examples of later architectural styles, set in splendid gardens and parklands.

Royal Botanic Gardens, Kew★★★
Over 40 000 species of plant are housed in the Victorian Palm House, the Temperate House, the Tropical Conservatory and the wooded grounds.

TRAFALGAR SQUARE TO BUCKINGHAM PALACE
The walk starts near Charing Cross underground station, and finishes near Green Park station.

Trafalgar Square★★
Trafalgar Square (EX), built over the former royal mews, commemorates the Battle of Trafalgar, the great sea battle between the English and French in 1805. Its victor, Admiral Lord Nelson, stands on **Nelson's Column**, 44m (145ft) high, guarded by four great bronze lions. On the north side is the **National Gallery★★★**. Behind, in St Martin's Place, is the **National Portrait Gallery★★**, with thousands of portraits of famous people throughout British history. On the west side is the church of **St Martin-in-the-Fields★**, rebuilt by Gibbs in the 18C.

The Square, with its attractive fountains, is a focal point for Londoners and visitors alike, despite the heavy traffic and the flocks of aggressive pigeons. During December

The statue of Nelson occupies a lofty position above Trafalgar Square, reputedly to allow the great man a view of the sea.

there is carol-singing beneath a large Christmas tree, given annually by Norway in gratitude for her liberation by British forces in the Second World War. Political marches often end here, with massed rallies, and on 31 December revellers gather to welcome the New Year.

Whitehall★★

Whitehall (EY) and Parliament Street are, in reality, a single thoroughfare which links Trafalgar Square and Parliament Square, cutting right through the heart of British

Looking along Whitehall at night, from Trafalgar Square; the light above Big Ben indicates that Parliament is still sitting.

political power. The name Whitehall recalls Whitehall Palace, the great royal palace that stood here from the 1530s to 1698. Its only surviving part is the **Banqueting House**★★ (built by **Inigo Jones** in 1622), which features a magnificent painted ceiling by **Rubens**. Through one of its first-floor windows Charles I walked onto the execution scaffold on 30 January 1649. When England's brief republican interlude came to an end in 1660, his son Charles II chose to celebrate the restoration of the monarchy at the Banqueting House.

One part of Whitehall was built on the site of a Scottish Royal Palace, and the names in this area reflect this, such as Great Scotland Yard and Old Scotland Yard.

Opposite is **Horse Guards**★, the official gateway to Buckingham Palace where a guard is mounted daily (*see* p.26). The archway leads to **Horse Guards Parade**, formerly the royal tiltyard, now a mere car park for civil servants. It is transformed each June, however, when the Trooping the Colour ceremony takes place.

Downing Street, closed to the public, consists of three elegant 18C town houses. No 10 is the office and residence of the Prime Minister. The Chancellor of the Exchequer lives next door at No 11, while the Government Chief Whip works at No 12.

The Cenotaph, bears the flags of the three armed services and the Merchant Navy and commemorates the nation's 'Glorious Dead' of the two world wars. The Remembrance Day ceremony is held here each November.

Government offices line each side of Whitehall, including on the right the Foreign Office and the Treasury, housed in imposing Victorian buildings.

The famous black door of No 10 Downing Street – home to the Prime Minister.

Cleaning the four giant clockfaces of Big Ben requires a good head for heights.

Parliament Square

If Whitehall is the domain of civil servants (state employees), Parliament Square (EY) belongs to politicians. The two **Houses of Parliament** are the Commons, which consists of elected Members of Parliament, and the Lords, largely made up of hereditary and life (appointed) Peers, and also the highest court in the land. Their home, the **Palace of Westminster★★★**, looks medieval, but much of it dates from the mid-19C when it was rebuilt after a disastrous fire. The only part surviving from medieval times is **Westminster Hall★**, which dates from 1097 and has a magnificent hammerbeam roof, crafted in 1394.

The Palace is flanked by the **Victoria Tower⋆** and the **Clock Tower⋆**. The latter houses **Big Ben⋆**, the world-famous bell; it is the first of Big Ben's chimes that signifies the exact hour. The Union Jack is flown from Victoria Tower when Parliament is sitting, and the Royal Standard flies once a year when the Queen opens Parliament. At night a light above the clock in the Clock Tower shows that Parliament is still sitting. The only parts of the Palace of Westminster open to the public are the Commons' and the Lords' Public Galleries.

Almost opposite Victoria Tower is the

Parliament Square is occupied by statues of former statesmen such as Winston Churchill, who keep a stern eye on proceedings in Parliament.

Jewel Tower, built in 1365 as the king's personal jewel store and treasury. Inside is a small exhibition of the history of Parliament. Almost adjacent is **St Margaret's Church★**, the parish church of the House of Commons. Winston Churchill, whose statue gazes towards the Commons from Parliament Square, was married here.

Westminster Abbey★★★

Every monarch since William I (except Edward V and Edward VIII) has been crowned in the Abbey, and many are also buried here, along with a host of other notables, including statesmen, artists, composers, writers and scientists. The lofty 13C nave is magnificent, with delicate stonework.

Although the nave of Westminster Abbey is relatively narrow, it is the highest in England (31m/100ft).

Henry VII's Chapel★★★ displays the banners of the Knights Grand Cross of the Order of the Bath, below the superbly vaulted ceiling. The **Chapel of St Edward the Confessor**★★ contains royal tombs and the oak Coronation Chair. In **Poets' Corner**★ are Chaucer's tomb and memorials to many great writers, though few others are actually buried here. Take time to stroll round the 13C and 14C cloisters and to visit the beautiful octagonal **Chapter House**, with its vaulted roof and fine tiled floor. The **Westminster Abbey Experience** provides a multi-media introduction to the Abbey's history and treasures.

The towers of the west front of Westminster Abbey, built in 1722-1745, were designed by Wren and Hawksmoor.

Royal Palaces

Buckingham Palace★★ (DY) is the most recent in a long line of royal London residences. Buckingham House, the original mansion on this site, was completely redesigned by the architect John Nash for George IV. Both George and his brother William IV died before work was completed, and even in 1837, when the young Queen Victoria moved in, the place was still unfinished. The east front was built in 1847 and its stone façade added in 1913.

Buckingham Palace is the weekday home of the Queen and the Duke of Edinburgh. Their apartment consists of some twelve rooms on the first floor of the north wing, with a view over Green Park. The Princess Royal (Princess Anne), the Duke of York (Prince Andrew) and Prince Edward also have apartments in Buckingham Palace. The Royal Standard flies when the Queen is in residence.

The Palace doubles as the operational hub of the Royal Family. Many of its 600-plus rooms provide offices for the large staff of the Royal Household – the people whose complex job it is to administer the affairs of the monarchy. Receptions and banquets take place in the State Rooms, and each year the Queen hosts three garden parties. The 28ha- (45acre-) gardens easily absorb the 8 000 or so guests who attend each party.

The **State Rooms**, with their rich collection of paintings and furniture, are open to the public from the second week of August to the end of September. At the side of the Palace, the **Queen's Gallery**, housed in the old chapel, stages changing exhibitions of paintings, drawings and jewellery from the Queen's collections. The gilded state carriages and coaches can be seen in the Royal Mews, where many of the Queen's carriage horses are stabled.

Kensington Palace★★ (BY) was the London home of the monarchy from 1689 to 1760 and Princess Victoria was living here before she ascended to the throne in 1837. Since 1760 it has been a residence for members of the royal family, notably the late Diana, Princess of Wales.

Buckingham Palace, with the Queen Victoria Memorial on the right.

The palace looks like a large country house, but inside there are some sumptuously decorated **State Apartments**, open to the public, and a large display of coronation robes and court dress.

The London apartments of the Prince of Wales (HRH Prince Charles) are in **St James's Palace★★** (DY) which is also used as offices for the Royal Household and for ceremonial occasions. It dates from the reign of Henry VIII (1491-1547), and from 1698 until 1837 was the monarch's principal official residence. Foreign ambassadors are still accredited to the Court of St James, even though they are received in Buckingham Palace.

Only the **Banqueting House★★** (EY) remains of **Whitehall Palace**, a vast royal residence built by Henry VIII, with more than 2 000 rooms, that once sprawled across the area between Horse Guards and the river. It burned down in 1698. Before Whitehall, the Palace of Westminster was the main royal residence and the centre of the court.

Kew Palace and Hampton Court are the other royal residences close to central London.

25

St James's Park was once a marsh, until Henry VIII drained the area and used it for hunting. Now, its colourful flowers and gardens are a popular spot for office workers and visitors. There are lovely views of the spires of Whitehall from the park.

St James's Park★★

One of London's prettiest parks, frequented by picnicking office-workers, St James's Park is roughly triangular in shape, with the Queen Victoria Memorial and Buckingham Palace (*see* p.24) at its west end. For centuries it was a royal park where monarchs and courtiers hunted, kept animals and birds (hence Birdcage Walk, the road along the southern edge), and enjoyed themselves. From the little bridge, there is one of London's most romantic views across the rooftops and spires of Whitehall.

Along Birdcage Walk (DEY) are the **Guards' Chapel**, the **Guards' Museum**, which recounts the history of the Foot Guards' regiments through displays of uniforms, weapons and memorabilia, and **Wellington Barracks**, where Guardsmen assemble before the Changing the Guard at Buckingham Palace. Along Horse Guards Road, on the park's east side, is the entrance to the **Cabinet War Rooms**, the fascinating underground headquarters of Churchill's War Cabinet during the Second World War.

St James's Park is a peaceful oasis in the heart of Royal London – in summer enjoy a lunchtime picnic.

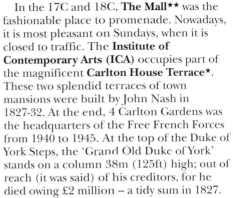

In the 17C and 18C, **The Mall★★** was the fashionable place to promenade. Nowadays, it is most pleasant on Sundays, when it is closed to traffic. The **Institute of Contemporary Arts (ICA)** occupies part of the magnificent **Carlton House Terrace★**. These two splendid terraces of town mansions were built by John Nash in 1827-32. At the end, 4 Carlton Gardens was the headquarters of the Free French Forces from 1940 to 1945. At the top of the Duke of York Steps, the 'Grand Old Duke of York' stands on a column 38m (125ft) high; out of reach (it was said) of his creditors, for he died owing £2 million – a tidy sum in 1827.

Several grand houses lead towards Buckingham Palace. **Marlborough House** is home to the Commonwealth Secretariat, **Lancaster House★** is used for official government functions, and **Clarence House** is the home of Queen Elizabeth, the Queen Mother. Sandwiched between them, the Tudor buildings of St James's Palace (*see* p.25) seem modest in scale. Behind is **Spencer House★★**, an opulent mid-18C palace, built for the 1st Earl of Spencer.

Changing the Guard★★

This ceremony, together with the Trooping the Colour (*see* p.19), provides the best introduction to the pomp and circumstance of royal London. The Queen's Guard is mounted at three different places: Buckingham Palace, St James's Palace and Horse Guards.

The most elaborate ceremony is at Buckingham Palace – 11.30am, daily from mid-April to the end of July, and on alternate days for the rest of the year. The proceedings last about 30 minutes. The

Guard, which is generally formed of a detachment of one of the five Foot Guard regiments, leaves Wellington Barracks in Birdcage Walk at 11.27am, to march to the Palace. (You can watch them forming up on the parade ground from about 10.45am.)

The St James's Palace detachment of the Queen's Guard marches to Buckingham Palace at 11.15am and returns to St James's at 12.10pm.

The Household Cavalry provides the Queen's Life Guard at Horse Guards from 10am to 4pm. The guard is changed daily at 11am, 10am on Sundays. The Guard leaves Hyde Park Barracks at 10.28am (9.28am on Sundays) and rides via Hyde Park Corner, Constitution Hill and The Mall. Every day at 4pm there is a ceremonial dismounting.

While the Buckingham Palace ceremony is the most spectacular, the sight of the Household Cavalry en route to and from Horse Guards is not to be missed.

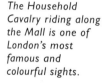

The Household Cavalry riding along the Mall is one of London's most famous and colourful sights.

THE CITY★★★
Start from St Paul's underground station.

St Paul's Cathedral dominates the City at night.

The 'Square Mile' is still the world's top financial centre, and on weekdays some 250 000 people work in the City's offices. In the evenings and at weekends, however, the streets are deserted, for only around 6 000 people live here.

St Paul's Cathedral★★★ and Barbican★
Today's City is the product of three relatively recent building booms: of the mid to late 19C, the mid 20C and the 1980s. Little remains of **Christopher Wren**'s City (*see* p.38) apart from St Paul's Cathedral, a few of his churches and the Monument in Pudding Lane.

Work on **St Paul's Cathedral★★★** (FX) began in 1675 and was completed in 1708.

Wren's great cathedral looms over the city, with the second biggest dome in the world. There are spectacular views across London from the exterior galleries.

Wren often clashed with the authorities about the design, both before work started and during construction, when he made radical changes. In 1697, Parliament halved his salary because work was proceeding too slowly, and he was not fully paid until 1711.

Baroque splendour characterizes the interior. The nave, dark at first, draws the visitor forward to the crossing, suffused with light, and then on to the choir, with fine wood carving and ironwork, and the High Altar. The magnificent dome frescoes are the work of Sir James Thornhill – Wren wanted mosaics. A stone set in the floor of the crossing marks Wren's burial place in the crypt. The inscription reads: *'Lector, si monumentum requiris, circumspice'* – 'Reader, if you seek his monument, look around.'

The former medieval alleyways between St Paul's and the river have many fascinating historical associations. In Wardrobe Place stood the Great Wardrobe, where medieval monarchs stored personal armour, robes and furniture. A Tudor theatre once stood in Playhouse Yard, and Shakespeare may have owned a house in Ireland Yard. **Apothecaries' Hall** in Blackfriars Lane is built around an elegant late 17C courtyard and is the headquarters of the Society of Apothecaries.

The dome of St Paul's has unusual acoustics: a whisper on one side can easily be heard on the other side.

A short way to the east, the steps of Peter's Hill descend to the river alongside the City of London Boy's School. There are fine **views** across to the reconstruction of Shakespeare's Globe Theatre (*see* p.67) and back to St Paul's.

Old Bailey runs from the far side of Ludgate Hill. The name actually denotes the street, but it is now usually used to refer to the Central Criminal Court, which

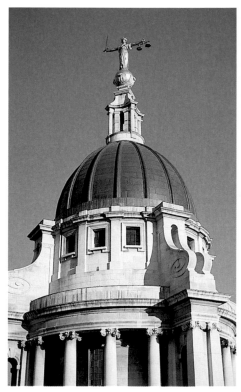

The gilded statue of Justice presides over Old Bailey, the Central Criminal Court.

dominates it. The court building, topped by the statue of Justice, scales in one hand, sword in the other, stands on the site of Newgate Prison where, until 1868, public executions attracted huge crowds.

High up on the corner of Giltspur Street and Cock Lane, at a spot formerly known as Pie Corner, stands the **'Fat Boy of Pie Corner'**, a gilded cherubic statue. He was erected to mark the furthest point reached by the Great Fire, and to remind the citizens of the sin of gluttony, which some religious zealots claimed had caused the fire.

St Bartholomew's Hospital (commonly known as Bart's) is London's oldest infirmary. It dates back to 1123 when Rahere, one of Henry I's courtiers, contracted malaria on a trip to Rome and vowed to build a hospital on his return. Rahere also founded a priory, of which the **Church of St Bartholomew-the-Great★★** is all that remains. This is one of London's oldest churches, with an atmospheric Norman chancel and nave. Its five medieval bells are the oldest complete ring in London.

Adjacent is **Smithfield**, London's main meat market, which opened in 1868. It has a suitably bloody history. Wat Tyler – leader of the Peasants' Revolt – was cut down here in 1381, and two centuries later Mary Tudor had 270 Protestants burned on the site. Smithfield's pubs open in the early morning, but only for the benefit of the market porters. Just beyond Smithfield, Charterhouse Square is a quieter spot graced with 18C houses. **Charterhouse★** (FV) was originally a 14C priory, then a famous school; now it is a home for elderly clergymen.

Outside the **National Postal Museum**

The Fat Boy of Pie Corner, marking the furthest extent of the Great Fire, warns against the sin of gluttony.

(which traces the history of the postal system, including stamps, delivery and uniforms), stands a statue to Rowland Hill, founder of the Penny Post. Opposite is one of the hidden gems that make London such a rewarding place to explore. The tiny square of **Postman's Park** features a wall of plaques commemorating ordinary people who died heroically in the act of rescuing or helping other people.

The **Museum of London★★**, a must for understanding the capital's development over the last 2 000 years, stands on the edge of the **Barbican★** development. This massive project was built in the 1960s and 1970s, and includes flats for about 4 000 people and the **Barbican Arts Centre**. Its concert hall is home to the London Symphony Orchestra, and the Royal Shakespeare Company (RSC) performs at its theatre for part of the year. The Barbican Art Gallery holds regular exhibitions of 20C art, and there is also a cinema. Follow the signposts carefully – it's easy to lose your way around in the Barbican, despite the system of coloured lines designed to guide you. At lunchtime you might seek out **The Vaults** pub in Chiswell Street, opposite the Whitbread Brewery.

The busy road named **London Wall★** extends along the site of the fortification first built round the City in the 2C (a piece of the original Roman wall can be seen in the

Half-timbered buildings above a 13C arch form the gatehouse to St Bartholomew-the-Great.

Museum of London). An elevated walkway runs past wall remains from the 17C and 19C and through Alban Gate, a huge office block (1987-92) with granite and glass towers. Descend to street level on the right (southern) side of London Wall, and follow Beaver Hall Gardens and Aldermanbury to the **Guildhall Library and Clock Museum★**. The small Clock Museum has some 700 fascinating historical time-pieces. Walk around the building and you will come to the main entrance to the Guildhall.

The **Guildhall★** (EX) is the centre of the City's unique system of government, which dates back to the 12C. The huge central Hall

Despite many changes, the Guildhall has remained the City's administrative centre since the 12C.

(*open to the public*) is decorated with banners and arms of the City Livery Companies (the predecessors of the City Guild Companies) and the figures of Gog and Magog, two legendary giants. Each November, the Lord Mayor's Banquet is held here to honour the outgoing Lord Mayor.

The remains of London's **Roman amphitheatre** were discovered in front of the Guildhall in 1988, and are now open to the public.

South of Guildhall lies Cheapside, medieval London's main shopping centre (*ceap* is Old English for 'market'). Milk was sold in Dairy Street, fish in Friday Street (Friday was a meat-free day), and shoes were mended in Cordwainer Street.

The bells of Wren's elegant but much restored **St Mary-le-Bow★★** are those within whose sound you must be born to qualify as a true Cockney (or so they say). It was also their chimes which supposedly persuaded the young Dick Whittington to 'turn again', and go back to London to fulfil his destiny by becoming Lord Mayor of London.

Ironmonger Lane and St Olave's Court are characteristic narrow City streets. Wren's **St Margaret Lothbury Church★** features elaborately carved woodwork, though the building is now overshadowed by the blank rear façade of the Bank of England (*see* p.43). Throgmorton Street used to throng with dealers making their way to the floor of the Stock Exchange, but nowadays share-trading is electronic and much of the atmosphere has disappeared.

Ahead is the **National Westminster Tower**, built in 1981 but badly bomb-damaged by the IRA in 1993. At 183m (600ft), it was the City's tallest building, now superseded by

Canary Wharf Tower, the pride of
Docklands, which is 251m (824ft) high
(*see* p.75).

Across London Wall lies **Broadgate**. This
mammoth development (built 1984-91),
which spans Liverpool Street Station,
consists of 13 buildings and three squares
and is mostly devoted to office space. An
open-air ice rink, sculptures, restaurants and
bars humanize the scale of the complex, and
frequent outdoor events draw the crowds at
lunchtime.

*The open areas of
Broadgate become
a hive of activity
when office workers
emerge for their
lunch breaks.*

Wren's London

The Great Fire of 1666 offered Christopher Wren (1632-1723) the chance of a lifetime. While the embers were still smouldering, Wren – a mathematician and professor of astronomy at Oxford – presented to King Charles II his reconstruction scheme for the City. Wren's vision of the new London was utopian: a geometric grid of intersecting avenues, with a triumphal arch, piazzas and a grand terrace along the river.

Vested property interests and inability to expropriate on a large scale prevented his plans from being implemented. However, Wren was appointed Surveyor-General to the King's Works, with responsibility for rebuilding **St Paul's Cathedral ★★★** (*see* p.29), and 51 new parish churches (to replace the 87 destroyed in the Fire, financed largely by a coal tax). The churches all had clear glass windows so the wood carvings, ironwork and painted altarpieces appeared to best effect.

The distinct steeples – elaborate creations in stone or lead, often multi-storeyed – are the hallmark of Wren's churches. Their designs varied essentially to identify the different parishes. While the churches were largely complete by 1685, the steeples were further embellished when more money was available, to complement the dome of St Paul's and create a majestic City skyline.

Wren's churches have suffered badly. Many of those

that were not pulled down – 19 were destroyed between 1782 and 1939, often to clear space for new offices – were bombed during the Second World War. The survivors, now dwarfed by office blocks, provide welcoming places of retreat for City workers and visitors. Some of the finest survivors are **St Bride's★** (p.60), **St Clement Danes★** (p.58), St Margaret Pattens (p.40), **St Mary-le-Bow★★** (p.36), **St Stephen Walbrook★** and **St Mary-at-Hill★★** (p.40).

Wren's other buildings include **St James's Church★★** (p.51) the **Royal Hospital★★** at Chelsea (p.76), the **Royal Naval College★★** at Greenwich (p.89), the State Apartments at **Hampton Court Palace★★★** (p.91), and **Kensington Palace★★** (p.24)

The Royal Naval College, Greenwich, one of Wren's great buildings.

From Monument to Bank★

The **Monument★**, topped by a gilded flaming urn, commemorates the Great Fire of London. It stands exactly 62m (202ft) from the house in Pudding Lane where the fire started on 2 September 1666, laying waste 80 per cent of the City. Over three hundred steps lead to the top, for views over the City (though somewhat restricted now by building development).

Beyond Pudding Lane turn left into St Mary-at-Hill. As you turn, look ahead to the old Billingsgate Fish Market, now redeveloped into a securities market with a huge dealing hall; the wholesale fish market has moved to Docklands.

Until a disastrous fire in 1988, **St Mary-at-Hill Church★★** was one of the best-preserved of Wren's City churches. The cool interior, with its elegant plasterwork, has been partly restored. Another Wren church, **St Margaret Pattens**, stands on the far side of Eastcheap. The roof of one of its canopied pews bears the monogram 'CW' (Christopher Wren).

Three great bronze horses stand in front of the massive **Minster Court** (built 1988-91) in Mincing Lane, which provides office space for no less than 5 000 people. The architects used a combination of pitched roofs, spiky façades and complex patterns to make the building seem modern, while still relating to the architecture of the past.

Dunster Court, London Street and New London Street take you past the 15C tower of All Hallows Staining to **St Olave's Church★**, which pre-dates the Great Fire. The famous diarist **Samuel Pepys** (1633-1703), who lived round the corner in Seething Lane, is buried here.

From Crutched Friars there is a view of

the Tower of London down Cooper's Row.
Jewry Street leads to Aldgate, a busy traffic
junction poised between the wealth of the
City and the deprivation of the East End.

Houndsditch is so called because dead
dogs, along with other rubbish, used to be
thrown into a ditch here. Concealed in a
small courtyard off Bevis Marks is the
Spanish and Portuguese Synagogue,
constructed in 1701.

St Mary Axe leads past the P&O and
Commercial Union buildings, among the
best of the City's 1960s structures, to the
controversial headquarters of **Lloyd's of
London★★**. Designed by Richard Rogers in
1986, the building has six satellite towers
with exposed metal pipework and a vast 61m
(200ft) glass barrel vault. At night from the

*The futuristic
façade of Lloyds of
London.*

Thames bridges floodlighting turns it into a gleaming electric-blue landmark.

The Victorian glass-and-cast iron building of **Leadenhall Market** dates from 1881, although the market, which specializes in meat and poultry, can be traced back as far as the 14C. Wine bars and restaurants now jostle with butchers and general shops. At lunchtime or early evening, have a drink with market traders in brightly-coloured jackets in **The Lamb Tavern** – a classic City pub.

Across Gracechurch Street, you plunge into a network of narrow passages. Bell Inn Yard leads to George Yard, with a modern water feature. The **Jamaica Wine House** (now a pub) in St Michael's Court was opened as a coffee house in 1688 and was patronized by merchants involved in the West Indies trade. Alternatively, try the **George and Vulture** or **Simpson's Tavern**, both time-honoured eating houses, which are close by.

Lombard Street, named after the North Italian merchants and bankers who settled in London in the 13C, is flanked by banks. As you walk along the street, take a moment to look up and see the range of signs still hanging outside the buildings. Tucked in the corner of Lombard and King William Streets is **St Mary Woolnoth**, built by Nicholas Hawksmoor (Wren's pupil) in 1716-27; the

The Jamaica Wine House is a popular watering hole for workers in the City.

austere exterior gives no hint of the rich interior, with its notable plasterwork.

At the very heart of the City (to the left) stands **Mansion House★**, the official residence of the Lord Mayor of London. The **Lord Mayor's Show★★**, the annual ceremony renowned for its pagaentry, starts from here in November. To the right stands the **Royal Exchange★**. The present building dates from 1838. Ahead looms the fortress-like façade of the **Bank of England** which, among other functions, designs, prints and issues banknotes and stores the nation's gold reserves. You can get a idea of the present workings and the 300-year history of this institution, known as the 'Old Lady of Threadneedle Street', at the **Bank of England Museum★** (entrance on Bartholomew Lane).

The equestrian statue of the Duke of Wellington stands in front of the Royal Exchange, founded by Sir Thomas Gresham in 1566.

COVENT GARDEN✶✶ AND SOHO✶

This walk starts from Covent Garden tube station and finishes near Tottenham Court Road station.

Covent Garden✶✶

There's a real buzz about Covent Garden, with its fashionable boutiques and stalls selling a huge variety of crafts from all round the world. There is a wealth of lively cafés, pubs, restaurants and nightspots popular with Londoners as well as tourists, and some first-class street entertainment, too.

As its name suggests, Covent Garden (EX) started life as a convent (market) garden, supplying produce for the monks of Westminster Abbey. It subsequently became London's main wholesale fruit and vegetable market and remained so for many centuries. The traders moved out in 1974 and, after something of a fight – there were plans to redevelop the area with high-rise office blocks – the area gradually took on its present character.

Street entertainers from all over the world enthrall the crowds at Covent Garden.

Some of the craft items on sale in Covent Garden make good gifts and souvenirs.

The **Central Market**, full of busy shops and trendy bars and cafés, is still Covent Garden's hub. On the west side, the portico of **St Paul's Church★** provides an informal performance space for street entertainers. This is where Professor Higgins first saw Eliza Doolittle selling flowers in *Pygmalion* and *My Fair Lady*. The peaceful churchyard (entered from King Street) leads to a simple Palladian building designed by Inigo Jones. It is famous as 'The Actor's Church', where many theatrical personalities are commemorated. On the south side, **Jubilee Market** features craft stalls and a weekly flea market, and there are more stalls in the main market building. Almost next door is

The Royal Opera house has hosted many of the world's leading dancers and singers.

the **London Transport Museum★** (EX), which tells the story of the capital's buses, trams and underground railway through historic vehicles and hands-on exhibits.

Covent Garden has always had close links with the theatre and the **Theatre Museum** contains fascinating exhibits and memorabilia of all the major performing arts.

The handsome **Royal Opera House★**, built in 1858, is home to the internationally famous Royal Opera and Royal Ballet companies.

North of the Central Market, there are particularly interesting shops in Acre Lane and Neal Street, while former warehouses in Shelton Street house fashionable galleries and salons catering for health, fitness and beauty. Neal's Yard Dairy in Short's

Gardens is packed full of unusual British cheeses. Around the corner is **Neal's Yard★**, a greenery-filled courtyard with several wholefood cafés, organic produce shops and interesting specialist shops.

Soho★

Two celebrated routes cross at Cambridge Circus. **Charing Cross Road** is famous for its bookshops, new and secondhand, while **Shaftesbury Avenue** is the heart of London's Theatreland. Gerrard Street, the centre of **Chinatown**, is entered through oriental archways, and has Chinese restaurants galore.

To the south lies the very commercialized **Leicester Square★** (EX), with its large cinemas, chain restaurants and mainstream nightclubs. The square has the Half-Price Ticket Booth (selling theatre tickets) and contains statues of Shakespeare and Charlie

Gerrard Street, the thriving heart of Chinatown.

Chaplin, as well as street entertainers and artists.

Soho★, bordered by Regent Street, Charing Cross Road, Shaftesbury Avenue and Oxford Street, has long enjoyed a dubious reputation. Nowadays, most (though not all) of the disreputable clip-joints and sex establishments have vanished, but Soho remains the centre of the capital's nightlife, packed with clubs, bars, pubs, restaurants and revellers.

This is also an enjoyable area to explore by day. There are numerous small art galleries, music shops, food shops and, especially around Old Compton Street, some delicious pâtisseries. The area is also the centre of London's trendiest gay scene.

On the west side, towards Regent Street, lies **Carnaby Street** – the centre of 'Swinging London' in the 1960s. Today it's very touristy and contrived, but fun all the same. Nearby, **Berwick Street Market** has been trading since the 18C and is full of colourful stalls selling clothes, fruit and vegetables. Wardour Street is the centre of the UK film and advertising industries.

Successive waves of immigrants helped give Soho its exotic character. The French Protestant Church in Soho Square is a reminder of the Huguenot refugees who first settled here in the 1670s, followed in the 19C by Greeks, Italians and Spaniards, and most recently by Chinese.

Some 18C and 19C houses survive in and around **Soho Square** and there is an especially handsome terrace dating from 1732 in Meard Street. In Greek Street stands the **House of St Barnabas**, an 18C house, simple outside but with a magnificent rococo interior.

A heady cocktail of different cultures, appealing to every taste and appetite – best go after dark.

ST JAMES'S TO MARBLE ARCH
The walk starts near Charing Cross underground station.

Berwick Street Market.

Pall Mall and St James's

Pall Mall runs west from Trafalgar Square (EX). Its curious name comes from *pallo a maglio* ('ball to mallet'), a croquet-like game that originated in France (despite its Italian name) and was all the fashion in London in the 17C. Nowadays, Pall Mall is dominated by **gentlemen's clubs**: the Athenaeum, the Travellers' Club, the Reform Club, the United Oxford and Cambridge University Club, and the Army and Navy Club, to name but a few. At No 107, the splendid classical-style **Athenaeum** building boasts a reconstruction of the frieze from the Parthenon in Athens.

The network of streets north of Pall Mall was first laid out in the 1660s. Proximity to the royal palaces and to Westminster meant that they soon became fashionable, and aristocrats, statesmen and diplomats set up their London homes here. The atmosphere is still exclusive, with numerous art and antique dealers. In King Street is **Christie's** auctioneers, founded in 1766, and next door is **Spink and Son**, dealers in art, silver, jewellery, coins and medals, founded in 1660. **St James's Square★** (DXY) also retains a number of elegant buildings. The gardens in the centre are open to the public and make a pleasant spot for a sandwich and a rest.

For at least a century, **Jermyn Street** has been the place to buy men's clothes and accessories. Famous names in this field include **Hilditch & Key** and **Turnbull & Asser**. Two other famous and picturesque old businesses along here are **Floris** perfumers at No 89, established in 1730, and at No 93 **Paxton and Whitfield**, London's oldest cheese store, established 1797.

Piccadilly★

At the eastern end of Piccadilly, the wide street leading to Hyde Park, is **Piccadilly Circus★** (DX), with the famous **Statue of Eros** at its centre. Two high-tech entertainment centres here attract young people of all nationalities. In the London Pavilion is **Rock Circus** (CDVX), Madame Tussaud's homage to the pop music industry, as wax models of stars are brought to life through animatronics. Almost next door, the centrepiece of the Trocadero Centre is the virtual-reality games arcade, **Segaworld**.

The major landmark along here is
St James's Piccadilly★, one of the few Wren
churches outside the City, and a masterpiece
it is. The sober exterior hardly prepares the
visitor for the graceful interior, with its
elegant woodwork and plasterwork. It stages
a lively programme of concerts and lectures
throughout the year. A few hundred metres
west, **Fortnum and Mason** is a temple to
gastronomy, with mouth-watering displays of
gourmet food and drink. On the splendid
clock above the entrance, figures of Mr
Fortnum (who was a royal footman at the
time of George III) and Mr Mason bow to

*Busy during the day,
Piccadilly really
comes alive at
night.*

The exclusive food emporium Fortnum and Mason dispatches goods in a horse-drawn van.

The restrained elegance of Burlington Arcade is relaxed a little at Christmas time.

one another on the hour. Their sumptuous afternoon tea is a favourite with many visitors; alternative venues in the area include Brown's Hotel in Albermarle Street or The Ritz further along Piccadilly (although you have to book well ahead to experience the luxurious ambience of the latter).

Opposite Fortnum and Mason is **Burlington House**, the sole survivor of several noble mansions built along Piccadilly in the 1660s. Learned societies occupy the wings on each side of the courtyard and the **Royal Academy** is housed in the central block, which retains some fine Palladian rooms. Major Fine Art exhibitions are held here throughout the year, including the celebrated **Summer Exhibition** featuring work by contemporary artists.

Burlington Arcade★, built in 1819, is patrolled by uniformed beadles whose job it is to maintain order: not an onerous task, one would think, since the atmosphere is always one of decorous restraint. The Arcade's small shops sell high-quality jewellery, fine knitwear and leather goods.

The Royal Academy will acquire a new extension as the collections in the **Museum of Mankind★** in Burlington Gardens (at the end of the Arcade) are gradually returned to the British Museum.

Mayfair★

Bounded by Regent Street, Piccadilly, Park Lane and Oxford Street, Mayfair takes its name from the raucous fair that, from the late 1680s to the mid 18C, was held each May on the site of Curzon Street and Shepherd Market.

During this same period, Mayfair was built over with many grand houses, interspersed with narrow streets and mews which housed stables and coach houses, grooms and coachmen. Though there has been much rebuilding, many Georgian houses survive, and in the western half something of the old atmosphere remains. Mayfair's eastern half is devoted to shopping on the most elegant scale.

North of Burlington Arcade, **Cork Street** is renowned for modern art galleries, while **Savile Row** is a byword for men's outfitters; you can watch cutters at work through the basement windows. In **Bond Street★** there are galleries, jewellers, antique-dealers and haute couture designers. Famous names include Asprey's, Agnew's, the Fine Art Society (note the Art Nouveau shop front) and Sotheby's auctioneers. On the corner of Bond Street and Grafton street sit bronze figures of Churchill and Franklyn D Roosevelt.

A few fine 18C houses also remain in Albemarle Street and Dover Street. The **Royal Institution** in Albermarle Street houses the laboratory of Michael Faraday,

Antique silver shop on Bond Street.

Berkeley Square may not have any nightingales left, but it is still a delight on a sunny spring afternoon.

who advanced the science of electricity.

From **Berkeley Square** – where, as the song tells us, nightingales once sang – Curzon Street and Charles Street run west, each lined with attractive buildings. **Shepherd Market★**, off Curzon Street, is full of alleys with restaurants, cafés, food shops and stalls. In summer everyone sits outside, and there is a real Mediterranean-village atmosphere.

To the north, **Mount Street** was rebuilt in the 1880s and 1890s in a vivid terracotta brick. More smart shops – oriental carpets, art galleries, etc. – mingle with everyday shops for local residents. Mount Street Gardens is a delightful oasis where local children play. Around the corner in South Audley Street is the charming little 18C **Grosvenor Chapel**.

By contrast, the great bulk of the **American Embassy** (1958-61) looms over **Grosvenor Square** (DX). In the gardens are statues to Franklin D Roosevelt and to the Eagle Squadrons, commemorating the 244 US personnel who served in the RAF before the US entered the Second World War.

Marble Arch

A few blocks north lie the bustling department stores of Oxford Street, while to the west, across Park Lane, is the verdant, restful expanse of Hyde Park (*see* p.56).

Amid the frenetic traffic at the end of Oxford Street is another of London's

Speaker's Corner on a Sunday morning – an eccentric shrine to free speech.

famous landmarks – the imposing **Marble Arch** (CX). Designed by John Nash in 1827, this great triumphal arch stood outside Buckingham Palace, until it was moved here in 1851 because it was too narrow for the royal coaches. The only people allowed to ride through it are senior members of the Royal Family and the King's Troop Royal Horse Artillery.

At the top of Park Lane is **Speaker's Corner**, where on Sunday mornings devotees of every religious and political ideal try to convert the passers-by. They often draw a considerable crowd, but the conversion rate is low!

A short distance away, at the junction of Bayswater Road and Edgware Road, stood the **Tyburn Gallows**, for nearly 400 years London's main execution site. It is estimated that around 50 000 people were publicly hanged here until 1783, when executions moved to Newgate (*see* p.33).

One of London's famous red buses, seen through Marble Arch.

The Royal Parks

Central London's five main parks were all originally royal possessions, used for hunting as well as for more leisurely pursuits. They form a great green swathe across the centre of the city – crucial breathing-space for local residents, office workers and visitors alike.

St James's Park★★
(*Tube: St James's Park*)
Attractive lake with fountains, magnificent flower beds, bandstand.

Green Park
(*Tube: Green Park, Hyde Park Corner*)
The least varied park – but none-the-less a pleasant swathe of grass and trees. Tradition has it that the area was once a burial-ground for lepers, which is why flowers do not grow well, though there are lovely daffodils in spring.

Hyde Park★★
(*Tube: Hyde Park Corner, Knightsbridge, Marble Arch, Lancaster Gate*)
The Serpentine, a lake formed in 1730 by damming a river, is the main feature, with boating and swimming in the Lido. There are good views from the bridge. Speaker's Corner and Marble Arch are at the north-east corner.

Kensington Gardens★★
(*Tube: High Street Kensington, Queensway*)
Adjacent to Hyde Park, this is traditionally the most refined of London's parks, with nannies overseeing their charges. The main points of interest are the statue of Peter

Pan (by Long Water, a continuation of the Serpentine), the **Albert Memorial★**, the Flower Walk and the Round Pond. Kensington Palace stands at the western edge.

Regent's Park★★★
(*Tube: Regent's Park, Baker Street, Camden Town*)
The most varied of the parks. John Nash built eight villas in the park and handsome terraces on the east and west sides. On the southern side is Queen Mary's Garden and the Open-Air Theatre, where Shakespearean (and other) productions are staged in summer. On the north side is **London Zoo★★**, created in 1828. It has long been a favourite destination for families and visitors to London. The zoo also incorporates a major research centre. Beyond it is Regent's Canal, with a pleasant towpath walk from Little Venice to Camden Lock.

Ceremonial cannons in Green Park celebrate the Queen's birthday.

STRAND★, FLEET STREET AND THE LEGAL QUARTER

The walk starts near Temple tube station and finishes near Holborn station.

Strand★

Somerset House★★ (EX), a huge 18C residence, contains the **Courtauld Institute Galleries★★** (*see* p.83) and in the wing overlooking the Thames, the **Gilbert Collection**, one of the largest collections of silver and gold objects in the world. The courtyard has been remodelled to host cultural events in the summer.

The two churches marooned in the middle of the Strand are Gibbs' **St Mary-le-Strand** and Wren's **St Clement Danes★**. The latter claims to be the 'Oranges and Lemons' church of the nursery rhyme and its bells ring out this tune. The church was burnt out during the Second World War; it now serves as the RAF Church and is full of Air Force memorials.

Beyond stand the imposing **Royal Courts of Justice**, opened in 1882 after moving from Westminster Hall. Only civil cases are heard here (criminal trials take place at the Old Bailey, *see* p.33). Step across the road to **Lloyd's Bank** and admire the ornate hand-painted decorative tiles in the entrance and the banking hall.

The **Temple Bar monument** in the middle of the road stands on the site of one of the original gateways into the City of London, removed in the 1880s. Since Queen Elizabeth I passed through here in 1588, a brief ceremony has been enacted whereby the monarch stops to ask the Lord Mayor's permission to enter the City to conduct a ceremonial engagement. Permission is never refused, but the City sets great store by this symbol of its traditional independence from the Crown.

The Temple★★

Two of the four **Inns of Court**, Middle Temple and Inner Temple, lie between Temple Bar (FX) and the river. The Inns of Court originated in the Middle Ages as a training establishment for barristers, and even today remain responsible for legal standards and most training. To practise in the British courts, barristers must be 'called to the bar' by one of the Inns. Students must not only pass examinations but also eat a certain number of dinners in the dining hall of the Inn to which they belong.

The Temple Church was founded by the Knights Templar, whose 13C effigies can be seen in the nave.

During the working day, the atmosphere is hushed and secluded, broken only by a bustle at about 4pm as bewigged and black-gowned barristers stream back to their offices (chambers) after the Law Courts rise. The names of the barristers belonging to each set of chambers are handpainted on boards outside. Take time to wander through; **Fountain Court**, **Crown Office Row** and the **Temple Church★★** are all worth seeing. The latter was built by the Knights Templar (from whom the area takes its name) in 1185. It has been much restored, but is famous for its unusual circular floor plan.

The beautifully maintained lawns of Inner Temple Gardens run down to the Embankment. In **King's Bench Walk** tall red-brick houses, designed by Christopher Wren, stand around a wide square.

Pass through the gateway into Tudor Street and street names reveal the history that lies beneath the pavements. In the Middle Ages, a large priory stood on Whitefriar Street and Carmelite Street. Down-river lay **Bridewell**, originally a palace built for Henry VIII, later a prison.

Fleet Street

Most of the country's national newspapers were written and printed in Fleet Street and its immediate environs until 1985. They had to move to offices that were better adapted to new technology, but you can still see the headquarters of the former *Morning Post* – where Churchill worked as a young man – on Aldwych Avenue, a semicircle connecting the Strand to Fleet Street, now converted into a luxury hotel, the *One Aldwych*.

It's not surprising that **St Bride's Church★**

In 1610 this fine half-timbered building on Fleet Street was a tavern. It contains Prince Henry's Room, named after Henry, Prince of Wales, whose coat of arms and initials it bears.

(FX), whose spire peeks out from behind new office blocks, was called the Journalists' Church. With its four rows of arcades, each smaller than the one below, surmounted by an obelisk, a ball and a vane, the **spire★★** is one of Wren's masterpieces. The church was badly damaged during the Second World War, but the bombing revealed the remains of a large Roman house, and of seven earlier churches on the site. Fragments of these are displayed in the church's crypt museum.

Wine Office Court leads past **Ye Olde Cheshire Cheese**, an atmospheric 17C pub where many men of letters ate and drank. **Dr Samuel Johnson**, who compiled the first

definitive dictionary of the English language, lived at No 17 Gough Square, now **Dr Johnson's Memorial House Museum★**.

Narrow back streets bring you to Chancery Lane and then to **Lincoln's Inn★★** **(FX)**, another of the Inns of Court, via a rear entrance in Bishop's Court. There are some lovely buildings here: the Tudor Old Buildings, the Chapel (which may have been designed by Inigo Jones in 1623), and New Square, a fine late-17C grouping.

Lincoln's Inn Fields is an attractive garden square surrounded by elegant 18C houses. One of them, nos 12-14, decorated with statues, was occupied from 1792-1837 by **Sir John Soane**, an architect and art collector. It houses the **Sir John Soane's Museum★★**, a highly eclectic collection where ancient friezes, Egyptian sarcophagi, paintings by Hogarth and Canaletto, Greek and Roman statues, Chinese vases and clocks are all mixed together, in a fabulously crazy jumble!

The intricately vaulted ceilings of Lincoln's Inn Chapel crypt.

THE THAMES AND SOUTH OF THE RIVER

This walkway runs alongside the river from Lambeth Bridge to Tower Bridge.

From Waterloo Bridge there is an unrivalled and dramatic view of the City.

Since Romans times, the north bank of the Thames has been the centre of political and economic power. Except for Southwark, the south bank remained rural until the 17C. After becoming an industrial area in the 18C, today it is the focus of major urban and cultural development, making the South Bank waterfront a very trendy area, while the streets beyond it have retained their traditional appearance. The **Queen's Walk**, a pedestrian walkway alongside the river, goes to **Tower Bridge** and provides magnificent views of the cityscape across the water, while giving you a look at the newer facilities.

Lambeth Bridge to Westminster Bridge★
Located on the south bank, at the south end of Lambeth Bridge, **Lambeth Palace** (EY) is the residence of the Archbishop of Canterbury. This palace with its red brick buildings, although highly composite, nonetheless has a certain appeal. Don't miss the delightful **Museum of Garden History**, located in the old church of St-Mary-at-Lambeth, whose former cemetery is now occupied by a reconstructed 17C garden.

Following the Thames, across from the Palace of Westminster, you pass in front of St Thomas's Hospital and on to the **Florence Nightingale Museum**, devoted to the nurse's life and work. It features a reconstructed hospital ward from the Crimean War period (1854).

The current **Westminster Bridge★** dates from 1862, when it replaced the 1750 version that was the second stone bridge across the Thames. At its far end, the **South Bank Lion** made of Coade Stone (an artificial, weatherproof stone formerly manufactured here) stands guard at the corner of Westminster Bridge Road, which you can take to visit the **Imperial War Museum★**.

County Hall★, an imposing building on the riverbank, was once the headquarters of the Greater London Council, disbanded in 1986. Two hotels were built in part of the building in 1998, while the façade overlooking the river leads to the **London Aquarium** where 30 000 specimens represent 350 species in natural underwater settings recreating the Atlantic and Pacific Oceans. The left-hand side of the façade houses the ticket office for London's big new attraction, the **British Airways London Eye**.

This huge wheel, situated along the river

The crenellated Tudor gatehouse of Lambeth Palace was built in 1485, though some parts of the palace date back to the 13C.

in the Jubilee Gardens, provides a 135m-(440ft-) high view of London inside capsules that take 30 minutes to go all the way round (*reservations essential* ☎ **0870 5000 600**). Weather permitting, you'll have a panoramic view of London that is unforgettable!

At the foot of the wheel lies Waterloo Pier, where you can embark on a cruise of the Thames all the way to Greenwich.

The path along the Embankment offers a fine view of the southern side of the Palace of Westminster.

South Bank Arts Centre★★

Beyond the iron bridge leading to Charing Cross Station (jazz-lovers will enjoy *The Archduke*, a café-restaurant located under the arcades), the walkway takes you to the **South Bank Arts Centre★★** (EFX), a cluster of cement buildings housing concert halls (**Royal Festival Hall★**, **Queen Elizabeth Hall** and **Purcell Room**), galleries (the **Hayward Gallery**, recognisable from the neon sculpture crowning it and where contemporary art exhibitions are held), the

The stark, modern architectural style of the Hayward Gallery has been much debated over the years.

National Film Theatre whose café is very popular, the **Museum of the Moving Image★** or **MOMI** (devoted to film and television), and theatres (the **National Theatre** and its various houses), while book-sellers display their wares on the waterfront.

The **BFI London IMAX Cinema**, accessible through an underground passageway, presents 2D and 3D films in a movie theatre that has nearly 500 seats.

Waterloo Bridge

Spanning a bend in the river, the bridge, built in 1945, offers a superb **panorama** of the heart of London (*see* p.63). On the right lies the spectacular skyline of the City, with the dome of St Paul's Cathedral, the futuristic lines of the Lloyd's Building and the **spire★★** of **St Bride's**. On the left, Big Ben looms over the Palace of Westminster, while the imposing terrace of Somerset House in front of you contrasts with the austere outline of the South Bank Arts Centre.

Stroll along the banks of the Thames among the craftsmen's workshops at **Gabriel's Wharf**, which is currently being redeveloped and is a particularly lively place during the Coin Street Festival in summer.

Oxo Tower Wharf was remodelled to accommodate low-cost housing, studios for designers, and a café-bar, as well as the **Oxo Tower restaurant** and **Oxo Tower Brasserie** located on the 8th floor of the building, providing a superb view of the city.

The walkway hugs the river below the Oxo Tower buildings (art galleries and design boutiques), and the majestic Sea Containers House, then runs under **Blackfriars Bridge** (FX) before reaching Bankside.

Bankside★

Situated right after the bridge, the **Bankside Gallery** holds regular exhibitions of contemporary watercolours and prints. It precedes the huge building of the **Bankside Power Station**, remodelled and lit up by a glass window, which now houses the **Tate Modern**, a fabulous museum of contemporary art featuring all the great 20C artists including Picasso, Matisse, Henry Moore, Francis Bacon and Andy Warhol…soon to be joined by future artists of the 21C!

The **Millennium Bridge**, a sparkling steel footbridge spanning the Thames, built by Sir Norman Foster in 2000 and decorated with a sculpture by Sir Anthony Caro, gives pedestrians direct access to the north bank

Discover your own London by walking along the South Bank from Westminster Bridge to London Bridge, remembering that all you see – St Paul's, Shakespeare's Globe, the great commercial buildings, are all in some way the gift of old father Thames.

The 17C George Inn once had galleries on three sides, so customers could watch plays in the cobblestoned courtyard below. Plays are still performed during the summer, along with traditional dancing and entertainment.

at the level of St Paul's Cathedral.

After going past the 18C houses along Cardinal's Wharf, you'll reach the **Globe Theatre★**, a half-timbered, circular construction rebuilt according to the original layout of the theatre that was destroyed in 1644. From May to September, classical plays are performed in daylight – keep your fingers crossed that it doesn't rain – with minimal sets, as in Shakespeare's day. If you're not lucky enough to attend a performance, you can still visit through the **International Shakespeare Globe Centre**.

Back on your way, you'll reach the heart of **Southwark** (FY), London's oldest suburb. In the Middle Ages it was an ill-famed area with brothels, theatres and bear-pits. The Bishops of Winchester owned many of these establishments, from which they earned a substantial income. Take Clink Street, under the railway viaduct, to get to the **Clink Prison Museum**, which affords a very realistic picture of Southwark's seven prisons. A bit further along, observe the vestiges of **Winchester Palace**, where the bishops lived, before reaching St Mary Overie Dock. There you can visit a replica of the **Golden Hinde**, the galleon aboard which Sir Francis Drake followed Magellan's path in 1577. Opposite it, overlooking the Thames, is the **Old Thameside Inn** where you can relax on the terrace. But the most beautiful monument in Southwark is its remarkable **cathedral★** (GY) begun in 1206, which will house an exhibition on the agitated history of this suburb once renovations are completed.

HMS Belfast and Tower Bridge at sunrise.

London Bridge★ to Butler's Wharf

Until 1738, **London Bridge★** (GX) was the only bridge across the Thames. The bridge you see today is not the original (moved ... to Arizona!), but rather a new structure built in 1972. Take a few steps onto the bridge to enjoy the view downstream of the elegant Custom House (early 19C), *HMS Belfast*, the Tower of London and the tall silhouette of Tower Bridge.

Continuing straight on from the bridge, Borough Hill Street takes you to Dickens' beloved Southwark inns, in particular the famous **George Inn★** (GY) built in 1676, of which the main building with its galleries subsists. Plays by Shakespeare are performed there in summer.

Hay's Galleria is often deserted during working hours but bursts into life at lunchtime and in the evening.

Returning to the waterfront, you will reach a series of former warehouses where goods from around the world were unloaded and stored in the 18C and 19C. The warehouses at **Hay's Wharf**, built in

The Neo-Gothic Tower Bridge was built in 1894. The lifting mechanism was operated hydraulically until 1976.

1857 to stock imported tea, have been converted into **Hay's Galleria** (GY), a very pleasant shopping mall giving onto the Thames. The huge atrium is decorated with a sculpture by David Kemp entitled *The Navigators*. There are many attractions in the area such as **HMS Belfast**, the Royal Navy's largest cruiser, now a floating museum ship, and **Winston Churchill's Britain at War** on Tooley Street (under the railway viaduct), a realistic reconstruction of life in London during the Blitz. Equally spine-chilling are the grim scenes on display at the **London Dungeon**! In the same morbid vein is the 19C **Old Operating Theatre** around the corner on St Thomas Street.

Despite its Neo-Gothic design, **Tower**

The famous Tower of London has held many an important prisoner within its dank walls, from Anne Boleyn to Rudolf Hess.

Bridge★★ (HY) was only built in 1894. The central span, designed to let tall ships through, only opens about ten times a week nowadays. It is a magnificent sight that has become quite rare when you think that the bridge was opened 655 times during its first month of operation! **The Tower Bridge Experience** is a small museum where you can learn about the bridge's history and the original hydraulic-lift machinery, as well as have a breathtaking **view**★★ from its upper-storey walkways.

From here there is a superb view of the **Tower of London**★★★ on the north bank (GHX). This fortress dating back to William

There are about 40 'Beefeaters', or Yeoman Warders, who guard the Tower of London.

the Conqueror (11C) was a prison for many famous figures facing a death sentence, such as Thomas More, Anne Boleyn, Lady Jane Grey, Sir Walter Raleigh and, more recently, Rudolf Hess. The Crown Jewels are held in this impregnable place in the **Jewel House★★★**, a dazzling collection of crowns, sceptres and swords. Look out for the ravens – legend has it that the day they leave the Tower, the Kingdom will fall! Luckily the **Yeoman Warders** ('Beefeaters'), wearing Tudor-style uniforms, are there to keep watch!

Crossing back to the south bank, enjoy a stroll through the former warehouses at **Butler's Wharf** where several restaurants have now opened up. The **Design Museum** holds temporary exhibitions that are sometimes very enjoyable. The **Bramah Tea and Coffee Museum★** traces the history of those beverages. If you feel like stretching your legs, why not continue the walk all the way to Greenwich?

Docklands⋆

London's docks were built in the early 19C to serve the massive trade passing through the world's largest port. Cargo ships brought in tobacco, spices, rice, wine, spirits, timber – and later, in the new refrigerated vessels, fruit, meat and grain before setting sail again with the products of Britain's booming manufacturing industries. The scene was set for 150 years of activity.

The 1960s and 1970s brought a sharp decline, and one by one the docks closed as new berths, equipped for modern container vessels, were built downriver. In 1960, there were jobs for 50 000 dockers. By 1985, only 3 000 remained, and 200 000 more jobs in dock-dependent businesses had vanished.

From the mid-1980s onwards, a massive redevelopment programme totally transformed Docklands. Aided by relaxed planning laws and substantial financial inducements, property developers found rich pickings in creating a new city to the east.

The largest projects were created on the Isle of Dogs, on the Thames' north bank, so named because hunting dogs were kept there. Development in Surrey Docks, on the south side, was on a more human scale, with more housing, especially for local residents. As well as over one million square metres of office space, almost 20 000 homes have been built and extensive leisure facilities, mostly water-based, created. The result is an exciting, modernistic but at times, alienating business environment, built in a variety of architectural styles.

The Island Gardens branch of the Docklands Light Railway (DLR) provides dramatic views as it swoops through the Isle of Dogs, often on stilts and crossing the three West India Docks on slender bridges. The first view of the water comes after Limehouse station; there is a marina in Limehouse Basin, and along the river are some 18C merchants' houses. Near Westferry station, the handsome Dockmaster's House has been converted into a restaurant.

Ahead is the huge **Canary Wharf complex**⋆⋆, the centrepiece of Docklands – if only by virtue of its size. Even the station, set under a vast canopy (most of the other DLR stations are bare platforms), seems cathedral-like. The office buildings are grouped around Cabot Square, where the computer-controlled fountain can perform 42 different water 'dances'. There are shops and restaurants at ground-floor and basement levels. Canary Wharf Tower – officially No 1 Canada Square – is visible from well outside London. At 272m (824ft), it is the tallest building in Britain and the second tallest in Europe. There are 50 storeys, 1.3 million square feet of office space, and 32 passenger lifts.

Crossharbour is the station for the London Arena, used for concerts and sports events, and for Millwall Dock, where great cranes stand along the water's edge, silent witnesses to history. Glengall Bridge is a swing bridge which admits craft to the dock near the entrance to the Thames; here, housing and small-scale offices are intermixed pleasingly.

Island Gardens station is close to the Thames. There are majestic views of Green-wich, reached by a foot tunnel.

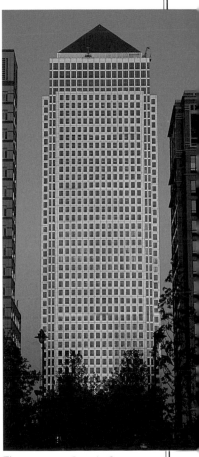

The tower on Canada Square dominates Dockland's Canary Wharf development.

OTHER AREAS OF INTEREST

Bloomsbury★
(Underground: Tottenham Court Road; Euston Square; Holborn; Goodge Street)
Beyond High Holborn and Bloomsbury Way lies a network of attractive little streets south of the British Museum (*see* p.82), lined with cafés, and book, antique and print shops. Near Holborn Tube is the excellent Princess Louise pub.

For many years, the handsome Georgian squares of Bloomsbury – the area running west to Tottenham Court Road, north to Euston Road and east to Gray's Inn Road – gained fame with Virginia Woolf and the Bloomsbury group: lawyers and teachers were also attracted to the area. Today, a number of terraced houses accommodate various faculties of University College, part of London University. **Bedford Square★★** (EX), Queen Square and Gordon Square are three of the most attractive surviving squares.

Chelsea★★
(Underground: Sloane Square)
The **King's Road** was a centre of fashion-conscious London in the long-haired 1960s and the spiky-haired late 1970s. It is well worth strolling along to see the latest fashions – and to be seen in them; Saturday is the best day. Fashionable boutiques still line the King's Road, alongside cafés, restaurants and antique shops.

A short walk away is the **Royal Hospital★★** (CDZ), founded by Charles II as a retirement home for veteran soldiers. Christopher Wren designed the buildings in 1692, and they remain largely unaltered. A dwindling number of **Chelsea Pensioners**, First World

War veterans, live here, recognizable by their distinctive scarlet frockcoats. The annual **Chelsea Flower Show** is held in the Hospital gardens, which run down to the river.

Nearby is the **National Army Museum★**, illustrating 500 years of British soldiering, in peace and war, through weapons, uniforms and other relics. By contrast, the neighbouring **Chelsea Physic Garden**, established by the Society of Apothecaries in 1676, is a peaceful haven.

Chelsea has always been popular with artists and writers, and in the late 19C acquired a bohemian reputation, counting Whistler, Rossetti and Oscar Wilde among its residents. There are many elegant houses in the streets and squares between King's Road and the river, most notably along **Cheyne Walk★** (CZ). **Albert Bridge★** is the most attractive of all the Thames bridges, with ornamented cast-iron work; it is delightfully illuminated at night.

The annual Chelsea Flower Show has become a place of pilgrimage for gardeners from all over Britain.

Knightsbridge** and Kensington**
(Underground: Knightsbridge; High Street Kensington; South Kensington)

These are two of London's smartest areas, with elegant shops and highly desirable dwellings. In Knightsbridge, **Harrod's** (CY) and **Harvey Nichols** are world-famous stores; there are also numerous boutiques on and around Sloane Street and Brompton Road.

South Kensington (BY) is famous for its three great museums – the **Victoria and Albert Museum***** (the 'V & A'), the **Natural History Museum****, and the **Science**

Harrod's exclusive department store is internationally acclaimed; here you can buy almost anything – at a price.

With 7 miles (11km) of galleries, the Victoria and Albert Museum contains one of the world's largest collections of fine and applied arts.

Museum★★★ – developed with the backing of Prince Albert, Queen Victoria's energetic and enlightened consort (*see* pp.82-85 for museum details). The great circular **Royal Albert Hall★** was dedicated to the memory of the prince and stages frequent concerts, including the famous eight-week summer season of Promenade Concerts ('the Proms'). Opposite the hall is the **Albert Memorial★**, a splendid expression of Victorian grandeur and self-confidence. An astounding £14 million was spent on restoring the Memorial to its former glory.

On the west side of Kensington Gardens stands **Kensington Palace★★**, London home of the Monarchy from 1689 to 1760, and still a residence for members of the royal family (*see* p.24).

Fashion boutiques and antique shops mingle with conventional chain stores along and around Kensington High Street. Just off

Queen Victoria dedicated the Royal Albert Hall to Prince Albert when she laid the foundation stone in 1868. Joseph Durham's statue of the Prince stands at the entrance.

the High Street are two distincitve Victorian houses. **Linley Sambourne House★**, the home from 1874 to 1910 of Linley Sambourne, political cartoonist and book illustrator, shows how life was lived in a prosperous Victorian upper-middle class household. **Leighton House★**, the home of the Romantic painter Lord Leighton, contains an exotic Arab Hall, with fantastic floral tiles and a fountain in the mosaic floor. Midway between these two houses is the **Commonwealth Institute★**, which contains displays on the history and culture of the 51 countries which make up the Commonwealth.

Spitalfields

(Underground: Liverpool Street; Aldgate East)
Spitalfields, in the East End, epitomizes London's cosmopolitan history. Large numbers of foreigners were already established here in the late 17C when a flood of Huguenot refugees arrived from France. Many were skilled weavers, and in the 18C they made Spitalfields renowned for its high-quality silks and tapestries.

The more successful settlers built elegant houses, some of which remain, notably in Fournier Street, Folgate Street and Elder Street; however, most lived in poverty-stricken conditions. In the 1880s, Spitalfields provided a haven for Jewish refugees from eastern Europe and Russia. It is now predominantly inhabited by Bangladeshis.

Spitalfields Market was established in 1682 and moved out to north-east London in 1991. The market building now houses a sports centre, restaurants and bars, craft shops, and a small opera house.

In recent years many artists, designers and craft-workers have settled in Spitalfields, converting the old weaving workshops into studios and bringing new life and vitality to the area. They sell their works from their studios and from small shops.

Brick Lane Market (*see* p.106) is well worth a visit; so too are the nearby shops and the curry houses, which are renowned as some of the most authentic and cheapest in London.

The imposing **Christ Church** (HX), built by Nicholas Hawksmoor in 1714-29, with a 68m (225ft) spire and a massive portico supported by four Tuscan columns, is being restored and is home to the **Spitalfields Festival** every June.

MAJOR MUSEUMS AND GALLERIES

*The **White Card** is a pass, valid for either three or seven days, giving entry to 15 of Central London's major museums and galleries. Family tickets are also available. Remember, though, that admission to the British Museum, the National Gallery, the National Portrait Gallery, the Tate Gallery, and a number of London's other top collections, is still free.*

The British Museum★★★

Great Russell Street.
Tube: Russell Square, Tottenham Court Road, Holborn (EX)

Founded in 1753 when Sir Hans Sloane left his collection to the nation, and established in its current building in 1850, this museum is getting a facelift by Sir Norman Foster. The previously inaccessible Great Court is going to be topped with a glass dome, while the rotunda inside the Court will house a variety of facilities such as the multimedia *Compass* programme, allowing more in-depth visits to the museum. The British Library reading room, formerly in the rotunda, has been moved to a new building in St Pancras. As for the fabulous collections, they are still displayed in over 90 galleries, so allow time to explore the many fascinating treasures. The most impressive permanent collections include those from Ancient Egypt, the Greek and Roman Empires, western Asia, Oriental Antiquities, and Roman and Medieval Britain. Highlights include the Rosetta Stone, the Elgin Marbles and the Sutton Hoo treasure, as well as the ethnographic collections which are gradually being returned to the

The Elgin Marbles can be seen at the British Museum.

Sainsbury Galleries after being exiled at the Museum of Mankind for 30 years.

Courtauld Institute Galleries★★
Somerset House, Strand.
Tube: Covent Garden, Temple (EX)
A world-class collection of Impressionist and Post-Impressionist paintings, including works by Monet, Renoir, Van Gogh, Cézanne and Gauguin, beside pictures by Rubens and Van Dyck and from the Italian school (14-18C) and British school (18C-20C).

Museum of London★★
150 London Wall. Tube: Barbican, Moorgate, St Paul's (FGX)
In a modern building at the corner of London Wall and Aldersgate Street, this museum is a must in order to appreciate the history and development of London. Innovative reconstructed interiors, shopfronts and important events in London's long history are included.

National Gallery★★★
Trafalgar Square. Tube: Charing Cross, Leicester Square (FX)
Housed in a rather austere 1830s neo-classical building, this gallery displays more than 2 000 paintings. Hung in chronological order, the paintings include many masters, from the early Italian Renaissance (particularly well-represented) to the 20C. Of special note are Leonardo da Vinci's *Cartoon*, *The Ambassadors* by Holbein, *The Arnolfini Marriage* by Van Eyck, *The Haywain* by Constable and Seurat's *Bathers at Asnières*. However, there are over 60 galleries, so allow time to explore.

The National Maritime Museum at Greenwich.

National Maritime Museum★★
Romney Road, Greenwich. Train: Maze Hill. River boat. Docklands Light Railway: Island Gardens, and cross river by pedestrian tunnel
Britain's seafaring heritage is celebrated in this 19C museum beside the Royal Naval College. Everything to do with ships is housed here, from tiny coracles to modern warships. Nelson's uniform worn at the Battle of Trafalgar (1805) is included, as are exhibits on Captain Cook's voyages. The Barge House has several impressive royal barges. Children will enjoy the **All Hands on Deck Gallery**, which allows plenty of 'hands-on' experiences of a nautical nature.

National Portrait Gallery★★
St Martin's Place. Tube: Charing Cross, Leicester Square (EX)
Housed in a 19C Italian-Renaissance-style building behind the National Gallery, this is the national collection of portraits of the great and famous. Over 5 000

The Natural History Museum.

paintings, sculptures and photographs are here, from Richard III to Margaret Thatcher! Also houses frequent temporary exhibitions.

Natural History Museum★★
Cromwell Road.
Tube: South Kensington (BY)
The magnificent 19C buildings were designed by Alfred Waterhouse in a Romanesque cathedral style. Look out for the numerous animal and plant motifs decorating the exterior. Inside are impressive displays representing the whole spectrum of the animal kingdom. The new Earth Galleries (replacing the old Geological Museum)

explore the formation of the Earth, its history through a time capsule journey, and minerals and geological formations. Always popular with children are the dinosaur displays. There are many other interactive and innovative exhibits explaining such subjects as ecology and human biology.

Science Museum★★★
Exhibition Road.
Tube: South Kensington (BY)
Near the Natural History Museum, the Science Museum contains five floors of wonderful exhibits tracing scientific research and development from early astronomy and medicine to modern space exploration. Many of the exhibits are interactive, so there are plenty of buttons for children to push.

Victoria and Albert Museum★★★
Cromwell Road.
Tube: South Kensington (CY)
This is one of the most comprehensive collections of the decorative arts in the world. Every aspect is covered in the 7 miles (11km) of galleries, including sculpture, furniture, fashion, paintings, jewellery, silver, metalwork, glass and ceramics. The 'V & A' has the largest collection of Indian art outside India itself. Look out also for the Dress Collection, which has examples of clothing from 1600 to the present day.

Tate Gallery★★★
Millbank. Tube: Pimlico (EZ)
Founded in the late 19C, the world-famous Tate has been renamed the **Tate Britain** following the opening of the **Tate Modern**

(*see* p.67) at Bankside. Devoted to British art from the 16C to 20C, from Constable to Hogarth, the Pre-Raphaelites and Turner (housed in an entire wing, the Clore Gallery). Round off your visit with lunch in the restaurant decorated with Whistler frescoes.

Wallace Collection★★★

Hertford House, Manchester Square.
Tube: Bond Street (DX)

This fine collection of paintings, French furniture and procelain was left to the nation at the end of the 19C. It is particularly rich in 17C-19C European art. Highlights include Frans Hals's *Laughing Cavalier*, and Titian's *Perseus and Andromeda* (both Room 22). It has an impressive armoury collection.

The Wallace Collection.

OTHER MUSEUMS AND ATTRACTIONS

London has a bewildering array of museums, historic buildings and attractions, encompassing almost every subject and catering for almost every interest. How many and which you choose to visit will depend upon individual preferences and the time available. Below is a list of those not described elsewhere in the guide.

Apsley House: The Wellington Museum

Piccadilly.
Tube: Hyde Park Corner (CY)

The former home of the Duke of Wellington (victor of Waterloo), it features his collection of paintings, porcelain and military decorations.

Barbican Art Gallery

Barbican Centre, Silk Street.
Tube: Barbican, Moorgate (GX)

Regularly changing exhibitions, featuring 20C artists.

Bethnal Green Museum of Childhood

Cambridge Heath Road.
Tube: Bethnal Green

The national collection of toys includes dolls' houses, puppets, children's costume, toy theatres and games.

Britain at War Experience

64-66 Tooley Street.
Tube: London Bridge

Vivid re-creation of London in the Blitz. Housed in a former underground bomb shelter.

BT Museum

145 Queen Victoria Street.
Tube: Blackfriars, St Paul's (FX)

History of telecommunications,

with old instruments and interactive displays.

Cabaret Mechanical Theatre

33 The Market, Covent Garden.
Tube: Covent Garden (EX)
Collection of contemporary
mechanical models.

Canal Museum

12/13 New Wharf Road.
Tube: King's Cross
Small museum of canal life, set in a
waterside warehouse.

Carlyle's House

24 Cheyne Row, Chelsea.
Tube: Sloane Square (CZ)
Memorabilia of the writer and
historian Thomas Carlyle, who
lived here from 1834 to 1881.

Chiswick House★

Burlington Lane, Chiswick.
Tube: Turnham Green
Beautiful Palladian-style country
mansion, built in 1729 for Lord
Burlington, with landscaped
gardens full of statues and follies.

Dickens House

48 Doughty Street. Tube: Russell
Square, Chancery Lane (EV)
Memorabilia of novelist Charles
Dickens, who lived here from 1837
to 1839.

Dulwich Picture Gallery★

College Road, Dulwich Village.
Train: North Dulwich, West Dulwich
Small but top-quality collection of
Old Masters.

Fan Museum★

12 Crooms Hill, Greenwich. Train:
Greenwich. Riverboat. Docklands
Light Railway: Island Gardens, and
cross river by pedestrian tunnel
Art, craft and history of fans, with
numerous artefacts.

Geffrye Museum★

Kingsland Road. Tube: Old Street,
Liverpool Street (GV)
Rooms in these 18C almshouses
are furnished to show changes in
domestic interiors from the 16C to
the 1950s.

Hayward Gallery

South Bank Centre, Belvedere Road.
Tube: Waterloo (EFY)
About four major exhibitions held
annually (no permanent displays).

Horniman Museum★

London Road, Forest Hill.
Train: Forest Hill
Fascinating collection of tribal
costumes, masks and other relics,
musical instruments, and botany
assembled in purpose-built Art
Nouveau building.

House of Detention

Clerkenwell Close. Tube: Farringdon
Prison life re-created in the underground remains of a 16C-19C gaol.

Imperial War Museum★

Lambeth Road.
Tube: Lambeth North (FY)
The story of 20C warfare. Plenty of
hardware, but also dramatic recon-
structions and displays on war's
social impact.

Jewish Museum

Raymond Burton House, 129-131
Albert Street. Tube: Camden Town
Artefacts and ritual objects related
to Jewish history and religion.

Kew Bridge Steam Museum

Green Dragon Lane, Brentford.
Tube: Gunnersbury. Train: Gunners-
bury, Kew Bridge
Massive Victorian steam-powered
pumping engines; working demon-
strations given at weekends.

London Planetarium★
Marylebone Road.
Tube: Baker Street (CV)
An introduction to the world of the stars and planets.

London Toy and Model Museum
21 Craven Hill. Tube: Bayswater, Lancaster Gate, Queensway (BX)
Large collection of historic toys and working models, including steam trains, aircraft and robots.

Madame Tussaud's★
Marylebone Road.
Tube: Baker Street (CV)
World-famous waxworks, with superstars, politicians, royalty, and a 'time-taxi' ride through historic London.

Marble Hill House★
Richmond Road, Twickenham.
Tube and train: Richmond
Beautifully restored Palladian mansion with river views.

MCC Museum
Marylebone Cricket Club, Lord's Ground, St John's Wood Road.
Tube: St John's Wood
Origins and history of cricket, plus tour of the ground, including the Long Room.

Musical Instruments Museum
368 High Street, Brentford.
Tube: Gunnersbury. Train: Gunnersbury, Kew Bridge
Vast collection of working mechanical musical instruments.

Osterley Park★★
Osterley, Isleworth. Tube: Osterley
Grand 16C country mansion remodelled by Robert Adam in the

A group of children learning about some of the paintings displayed in the Tate Gallery.

18C, with a fine collection of furniture and attractive grounds.

Pollock's Toy Museum
1 Scala Street. Tube: Goodge Street, Tottenham Court Road (DX)
Tiny atmospheric museum with dolls, teddy bears, puppets.

Rugby Football Union Museum
Gate 7, Rugby Football Union Stadium, Rugby Road, Twickenham Train: Twickenham
Rugby football memorabilia and a tour of the ground.

Thames Barrier Visitors' Centre
Unity Way, Woolwich.
Train: Charlton. River boat
Exhibition and views of the Thames Barrier, the world's largest moveable flood barrier.

Tower Hill Pageant★
Tower Hill. Tube: Tower Hill (GX)
A ride back through the history of London, with sensory effects.

Wembley Stadium Tours
Wembley Stadium, Wembley.
Tube: Wembley Park
A behind-the-scenes look at the 'cathedral of association football'.

Westminster Cathedral★
Francis Street, off Victoria Street.
Tube: Victoria (EY)
England's principal Roman Catholic church, built in neo-Byzantine style. There are good views from the tower.

Whitechapel Gallery
80 Whitechapel High Street.
Tube: Aldgate East (HX)
Regularly changing exhibitions, generally of contemporary artists.

Wimbledon Lawn Tennis Museum
Church Road, Wimbledon.
Tube: Southfields
Social and sporting history of tennis, with racquets, fashions and memorabilia.

The Millennium Dome seen through the Thames Barrier.

FURTHER AFIELD

Greenwich★★★

Whether you approach Greenwich, 8km (5 miles) east of central London, by river boat or take the Docklands Light Railway (DLR) to Island Gardens, then the foot tunnel beneath the Thames, you will see Greenwich as it is intended to be seen – from the river. Facing you are the majestic classical buildings of the **Royal Naval College★★**, designed by Christopher Wren (*see* p.39). The magnificent **Painted Hall★** and the chapel are open to the public. Sandwiched between the College buildings is the exquisite Palladian **Queen's House★★**, built by Inigo Jones in 1616 for Anne of Denmark, the queen of James I. Beautifully restored, it now features a large maritime art collection (buy your ticket first from the National Maritime Museum).

The meridian (0° longitude), which divides the earth into the eastern and western hemispheres, runs through the **Old Royal Observatory★**. A large red ball on a rod above one of the turrets drops every day at 1pm precisely (as it has done since 1833), to signal the exact time to sailors on the Thames. The building is now a museum of beautiful and complex instruments used to measure time and space through the ages.

It is fitting that Greenwich, the 'Home of Time' is the site of the **Millennium Dome**. The Dome, the largest structure of its kind in the world, houses the Millennium Experience, with exhibits and attractions exploring the choices facing mankind in the 21C. The colourful, allegorical Millennium Show features around 60 artists, combining special effects, music (notably by U2 and

Peter Gabriel) and acrobatic performances
in the air. Tickets are available from any
National Lottery game retailer or ☎ **0870
606 2000**. Alongside the Dome is the **Sky
Zone**, with two 2 500-seat cinemas for staging
films, concerts and other live events during
the year (*for information on getting to the Dome
see* p.119).

The three tall masts of the **Cutty Sark★★**,
the last of the clippers that carried tea from
China and wool from Australia, stand proud.
Next to her (and tiny in comparison) is
Gipsy Moth IV, in which Sir Francis
Chichester made his single-handed
circumnavigation of the globe in 1966/67.
For nautical matters, the **National Maritime
Museum★★** is probably the most
comprehensive collection of its kind (*see* p.83).

Hampton Court Palace★★★
Henry VIII's Lord Chancellor, **Cardinal
Thomas Wolsey**, began construction of this
sumptuous riverside residence in 1514. It
outshone even Henry's palaces, however,
and in 1529 Henry acquired it from the
disgraced Wolsey. The king extended the
house and gardens and came here to relax
from the court at Westminster, as did most
subsequent monarchs during the next three
centuries. In the 1690s, William and Mary
commissioned Wren for the final phase of
construction, the State Apartments.

The result is a mixture of some of the
country's finest Tudor and Classical
architecture. Look especially at the **Tudor
Great Hall** with its magnificent
hammerbeam roof, the ornate **Chapel
Royal**, and the **Astronomical Clock**. Made
for Henry VIII in 1540, the clock displays
the hour, month, date, sign of the zodiac,

Hampton Court Palace – weekend retreat of Henry VIII.

year, phase of the moon, and the sun revolving round the earth. Wren's **State Apartments** are luxuriously decorated, and include the Renaissance Picture Gallery, featuring some striking royal portraits.

The magnificent **palace grounds★★★** include formal Dutch-style gardens and parkland, originally royal hunting ground and still home to a herd of deer. Highlights are: the famous **Maze**; the enormous **Great Vine★**, which was planted in 1768; and the indoor **Royal Tennis Court** built in 1626, where the archaic game of Real Tennis is still played. In the **Lower Orangery** are displayed the *Cartoons of The Triumph of Caesar*, executed by Mantegna in the 1490s.

Kew★★★

Kew is the home of the **Royal Botanic Gardens★★★** (Kew Gardens), where 40 000 different species of plant are cultivated in glass houses that reproduce specific habitats.

Tropical plants thrive inside the **Victorian Palm House★★**. The elaborate **Temperate House★** contains camellias and rainforest trees; the route round the **Princess of Wales Tropical Conservatory** passes through ten separate tropical habitats, from swamp to desert. Scattered throughout the gardens, which run down to the Thames, are areas devoted to particular species, such as alpines, heathers and rhododendrons, as well as an extensive arboretum. Before the Botanic Gardens were handed to the nation in 1840 they were in royal ownership, and several monarchs and their queens helped to develop the plant collections and botanical research for which Kew remains renowned. There are several 18C follies, including an Orangery and a 50m- (163ft-) high Pagoda. **Kew Palace★★**, a handsome,

The tropical temperatures in the beautifully restored Victorian Palm House, Kew, enable you to enjoy the wonderful plants, even on a wet winter's day.

small, Dutch-style house which was once a summer home to George III and Queen Charlotte, is the only royal residence to survive at Kew. The **Queen's Garden**, behind the palace, is laid out in formal 17C style.

On the opposite bank of the Thames stands **Syon Park★★**, home of the Dukes of Northumberland since 1594. The house was remodelled on a grand scale by Robert Adam in the 1760s, with several ornate formal rooms. The outstanding **gardens★**, laid out by 'Capability' Brown, include a splendid conservatory, a garden centre and the **London Butterfly House**.

Richmond★★

Richmond retains its country town atmosphere. Handsome houses stand around Richmond Green and along Old Palace Terrace and **Maids of Honour Row★★★**. The gateway on the Green and part of the former Royal Wardrobe in Old Palace Yard is all that survives of **Richmond Palace**, a princes' residence from the 14C to 17C.

Richmond Bridge, completed in 1777, is the oldest surviving Thames bridge in London. Climb **Richmond Hill** for an extensive view of the Thames from the top, and then walk on into **Richmond Park★★**, originally a royal hunting ground, which today is home to some 600 deer.

Hampstead★

Set high on a hill 6km (4 miles) north of central London, Hampstead has managed to hold on to its village atmosphere. It first became fashionable in the early 18C; many artists, writers and politicians have lived here, imparting an intellectual reputation. This is reflected in the bookshops, antique shops, galleries and smart restaurants along the High Street and Heath Street. Behind here stand handsome squares with elegant mansions. One such is **Fenton House★★**, built in 1693, with fine displays of porcelain, and a collection of early musical instruments. **Keats House**, the home of John Keats between 1818 and 1820, contains mementoes of the brilliant young poet.

On the northern edge of **Hampstead Heath**, which provides superb views over central London, is **Kenwood House★★**. Enlarged by Robert Adam in 1769, it contains the superb Iveagh Bequest collection of paintings.

WEATHER

London enjoys a moderate climate all year round without any real extremes of temperatures, which remain a few degrees higher than those in the surrounding areas. However, the weather can be changeable and, especially in spring and autumn, a fair and sunny morning may turn wet and cold in the afternoon.

June is the sunniest month, with an average of over 8.5 hours of sunshine per day; May, July and August are not far behind. April and September are usually sunny as well, with a daily average of around six hours.

June is perhaps the most pleasant month to explore the city. It enjoys an average temperature of about 20°C (68°F) but is less humid than July and August.

The coldest months are December, January and February when the average temperature is about 5°C (41°F); November and March are only a slight improvement. Fog is no longer common since London is less polluted than in the 19C, but the air quality may be poor in certain atmospheric conditions. There is a chance of rain throughout the year, though the winter months are usually the wettest. Snow is a relatively rare occurrence in London.

Daylight hours are long in the summer. The sun rises soon after 5am and, around midsummer, does not set until almost 10pm: summer evenings are magical times for strolling, enjoying a pint in a pub garden or attending an open-air theatre.

CALENDAR OF EVENTS

Consult the London Tourist Board and the weekly magazine *Time Out* for information.

1 January London Parade – An American-style parade led by the Lord Mayor of Westminster, from Westminster Bridge to Berkeley Square.

2nd or 3rd week February Chinese New Year celebrations – Traditional celebrations including lion and dragon dances in Chinatown (Soho).

Late March/early April (Saturday before Easter) University Boat Race – Oxford and Cambridge universities' famous rowing race between Putney and Mortlake.

3rd Sunday April: London Marathon – run from Greenwich/Blackheath to the Mall in Westminster.

3rd week May (for four days): Chelsea Flower Show, Royal Hospital, Chelsea – An Internationally-renowned event, with imaginative garden designs and dazzling floral displays (last two days general public).

29 May: Chelsea Pensioners' Oak Apple Day Parade, Royal Hospital, Chelsea.

Early June to mid August: Royal Academy Summer Exhibition.

Early to mid June: Spitalfields Festival.

2nd or 3rd Saturday June: Trooping the Colour, Horse Guards – The Massed Bands and Troops of the Household Division troop their colours as the the Queen takes the salute on her official birthday.

Last week June, first week of July: Wimbledon Lawn Tennis Championships – International tennis tournament.

2nd half of June and early July: City of London Festival – Classical music performed by international players and singers in venues across the City, including many which are not usually open to the public.

Mid July to mid September: Henry Wood Promenade Concerts ('The Proms') – A celebrated series of mostly orchestral concerts at the Royal Albert Hall.

Mid to late July: Royal Tournament – Spectacular display of military skills at Earls Court Exhibition Centre.

Last weekend August: Considered Europe's largest street party, the Notting Hill

The Oxford team powers through Hammersmith at a rate of knots in the annual University Boat Race.

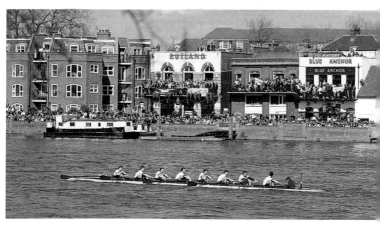

Carnival is two days of carnival parades and music.

Around 20 October: Trafalgar Day Parade, Trafalgar Square.

Late October/early November: State Opening of Parliament.

1st Sunday November: London to Brighton Veteran Car Run, Hyde Park.

Early November to 6 January: Christmas lights in Regent Street and Oxford Street.

Early to mid November: London Film Festival.

2nd Saturday November: Lord Mayor's Show, grand parade through the City with bands, floats, funfair and fireworks.

Sunday nearest to 11 November: Remembrance Service and Parade, Cenotaph, Whitehall.

Early December to 6 January: Christmas tree in Trafalgar Square. Carol-singing nightly until 24 December.

ACCOMMODATION

London's range of accommodation is enormous, from extremely expensive and opulent hotels to simple B&Bs (bed and breakfast). London is an expensive place to stay and it is worth shopping around. Check whether Continental or a full English breakfast and VAT (*see* p.120) are included. Single occupants usually fare badly, often paying nearly as much as

Fireworks illuminate the night sky over the Thames, the grand finale to the Lord Mayor's Show.

Dancing in the street – the colourful extravaganza of the Notting Hill Carnival livens up London's streets.

two sharing a double room.

As a rough guide, you can expect to pay £300 or more at a luxury hotel for a double room. Mid-priced hotels will cost around £100-150 per night, while moderate hotels charge around £100. The budget range hotels in the **Travel Inn** chain offer simple but comfortable rooms at a fixed rate per room (£62.95, for up to 3 people). Guesthouse prices are on a par with the cheapest hotels, although evening meals are not always served. B&Bs are about £15-£30 per person per night.

If you haven't reserved a room before arriving, the **London Tourist Board** will assist you (for a fee of £5). You can also contact the **London Tourist Board Hotel Booking Line** (a credit card booking service) at ☎ **020 7604 2890** (fee charged) or www.londontown.com.

On the same internet site, the **London Bed and Breakfast Agency Ltd**, 71 Fellows Road, NW3 3JY ☎ **020 7586 2768**, fax 020 7586 6567 offers B&Bs to suit all budgets in various London neighbourhoods.

Twenty 2- to 5-star hotels are grouped under one reservation agency (☎ **0800 402215**; www.london.hotels.co.uk), allowing you to choose according to your taste and budget from the prestigious hotels such as the Waldorf Meridian or the Strand Palace to the more convivial Posthouse and Travelodge hotels.

For those on a tight budget, the **Youth Hostels Association** of England and Wales has six hostels in London. YHA membership is required (there is no age limit) but this can be obtained on the spot; proof of your current address is necessary. Further details can be obtained from the Member-ship and Booking Office: 14 Southampton Street, WC1E 7HA ☎ **020 7373 3400** or ☎ **020 7836 8541**. Cheap accommodation is also available at the **International Students House** (ISH), 229 Great Portland Street W1N 5HD, ☎ **020 7631 8300** (students only; single or double rooms and dormitories).

For information on hotels and restaurants, consult the *Michelin Red Guide London*, an extract from the annual *Michelin Red Guide Great Britain and Ireland*.

Recommendations
Over £150
The Hempel (*31-35 Craven Hill Gardens, W2* ☎ 020 7298 9000) Feel like a splurge? Try this striking hotel, famous since Julia Roberts got married here in the film *Notting Hill*!
Beaufort (*33 Beaufort Gardens, SW3 1PP* ☎ 020 7584 5252)

Friendly and comfy hotel on a quiet cul-de-sac in the fashionable Knightsbridge, halfway between Harrod's and the Victoria and Albert Museum.
Parkes (*41 Beaufort Gardens, SW3 1PW* ☎ 020 7581 9944) Situated close to the Beaufort.

£100-150
Hazlitt's (*6 Frith Street, W1V 5TZ* ☎ 020 7434 1771) Well-appointed town house in the heart of Soho.
Pembridge Court (*34 Pembridge Gardens*, W2 4DX ☎ 020 7229 9977) Smart and friendly town-house hotel near Portobello market.

Around £100
Knightsbridge Green (*159 Knightsbridge, SW1X 7PD* ☎ 020 7584 6274) Comfortable hotel just a few steps away from Harrod's.
Five Sumner Place (*5 Sumner Place, SW7 3EE* ☎ 020 7584 7586) and **Aster House** (*3 Sumner Place, SW7 3EE* ☎ 020 7581 5888) Two attractive town-house hotels offering good value in smart South Kensington.
Durrants (*26-32 George Street, W1H 6BJ* ☎ 020 7935 8131) A converted row of Georgian town houses conveniently situated just north of Oxford Street; traditional club ambience.

Hart House (*51 Gloucester Place, W1H 3PE* ☎ 020 7935 2288) Small family-run hotel with easy access to Oxford Street shopping.

Around £60

London County Hall Travel Inn Capital (*Belvedere Road, Waterloo, SE1* ☎ 020 7902 1600) Modern budget hotel with views of the Thames and the Houses of Parliament.

London Euston Travel Inn Capital (*141 Euston Road, Euston, NW1 2AV* ☎ 020 7554 3400) Modern budget hotel situated near to King's Cross and Euston stations.

Tower Bridge Travel Inn Capital (*159 Tower Bridge Road, SE1 3LP* ☎ 020 7940 3700)

Travelodge (*200 York Road, Battersea, SW11 3SA* ☎ 0800 850950 for freephone reservations) Modern lodge style; situated just south of the Thames.

Travelodge (*Coriander Road, off AB East India Dock Road, Docklands, E14* ☎ 0800 850950 for freephone reservations) Modern lodge style; convenient for the City of London, Greenwich and Millennium Dome. Ideal for those arriving by car, with its huge car park. Take the no 15 bus or Docklands Light Railway for the city centre.

FOOD AND DRINK

London has long been recognized as the ethnic eating capital of the world. Countless international cuisines are represented here. English cooking, too, is also enjoying an overdue renaissance.

Brasseries are informal all-day establishments where you can enjoy a full meal, or simply a dessert, a drink or a cup of coffee. London's **cafés** have also become increasingly stylish, many now serving a wide selection of coffees, croissants and pastries.

Pubs vary a great deal; some are excellent, some are dire. If you want to try London's own beers look out for Young's and Fuller's brews, but there are also interesting guest bitters from other breweries. Although many pubs serve predictable and uninspired fare, a good one is a unique London experience and a way of eating solid lunchtime fare at a sensible price.

The following suggestions offer a typical ambience, and are renowned for the quality of their food and beers:

The Queens *49 Regent's Park Road, Primrose Hill, NW1 8XE* Tube: Chalk Farm

Havelock Tavern *57 Masbro Road, Hammersmith, W14 0LS* Tube: Holland Park

Anglesea Arms *35 Wingate Road, Hammersmith, W6 0UR*
Tube: Ravenscourt Park
Peasant *240 St John St, Islington, EC1V 4PH* Tube: Angel
Chelsea Ram *32 Burnaby Street, Chelsea, SW10 0PL*
Tube: Fulham Broadway
Ye Olde Mitre Tavern *1 Ely Court, EC1* Tube: Chancery Lane
Seven Stars *Carey Street, WC2*
Tube: Holborn
Lamb and Flag *33 Rose Street, WC2* Tube: Covent Garden
Salisbury 90 *90 St Martin's Lane, WC2* Tube: Leicester
The Phoenix *Cavendish Square*
Tube: Oxford Circus
The Shakespeare's Head *Carnaby Street, W1*
Tube: Oxford Circus
The Bunch of Grapes *207 Brompton Road, SW1*
Tube: Knightsbridge
The Nag's Head *53 Kinnerton Street, SW1*
Duke of Wellington *63 Eaton Terrace, SW1* Tube: Sloane Square
The Anchor *1 Bankside, SE1*
Tube: Southwark
Old Thameside Inn *Bank End, SE1*
George Inn *77 Borough High Street, SE1* Tube: Borough
Blackfriars Pub *174 Queen Victoria Street, EC4*
Tube: Blackfriars
The George *213 Strand, WC2*
Tube: Aldwych
Devereux *20 Devereux Court,*
WC2 Tube: Temple
Gordon's Wine Cellar *Villiers Street, WC2* Tube: Embankment
The Churchill Arms *119 Kensington Church Street, W8*
Tube: Notting Hill Gate
The Grapes *76 Narrow Street, E14* Docklands Light Railway, station Limehouse
Dickens Inn *St Katharine Dock E1*

Wine bars offer a larger and more interesting selection of wines than pubs and a different atmosphere.

Where to eat

Covent Garden and Soho are fashionable eating areas, but there are interesting restaurants in every corner of the city.

There is a clutch of new restaurants along the South Bank, from the Festival Hall to beyond Tower Bridge. Chinatown, in and around Gerrard Street, is the best place for Chinese food. For Indian and Bangladeshi restaurants, explore Commercial Road or Brick Lane, or take a trip out to Wembley, also known as 'Little India'. Brixton is the place to go for authentic West Indian takeaway food. Greek restaurants abound in and near Charlotte Street. Good Italian restaurants and cafés can also be found in this area, as well as all over London. For Middle Eastern food, try Edgware Road.

Where to take a break? 'Elementary, my dear Watson,' – the Sherlock Holmes pub, near Scotland Yard.

Recommendations

Here are a few suggestions for restaurants arranged according to price: Very expensive (over £40), Expensive (around £30) and Moderate (under £30).

Very expensive

Gordon Ramsay *(68-69 Royal Hospital Road, SW3* ☎ *020 7352 4441)* Inventive cuisine in a very comfortable setting. Reservations essential!

The Oriental *(Park Lane, W1A 2HJ* ☎ *020 7317 6328)* Refined Chinese cooking in the luxurious setting of the Dorchester Hotel.

Bibendum *(81 Fulham Rd, SW3 6RD* ☎ *020 7581 5817)* A unique dining experience in the fanciful Michelin building.

Expensive

One-O-One *(William Street, Knightsbridge, SW1X 7RN* ☎ *020 7290 7101)* Fish is king here, but the young French chef also does traditional dishes.

Pharmacy *(150 Notting Hill Gate, W11* ☎ *020 7221 2442)* As its name suggests, medication is the theme of the decor in this bar restaurant. Drop in on this trendy spot, maybe just for a drink – perhaps an *Aspirin*, a *Viagra* or a *Prozac Fizz?*

Le Pont de la Tour *(Butlers Wharf, SE1,* at the foot of Tower Bridge ☎ *020 7403 8403)* Bar and grill, serving grilled meats, salads and shellfish. Next door, the **Butlers Wharf Chop House** *(*☎ *020 7403 3403)*, known for its steak and kidney pudding (with or without oysters!) also serves simple bar food. Both have terraces overlooking the Thames; booking advisable.

Simpson-in-the-Strand (*100 Strand, WC2* ☎ 020 7836 9112) Traditional English cooking and atmosphere in this famous 19C tavern.

Tate Gallery Restaurant (*Tate Gallery, Millbank, SW1P 4RG* ☎ 020 7887 8877) Contemporary British cuisine served in the museum's basement hall. Lunch only.

Rules (*35 Malden Lane, WC2E 7LB* ☎ 020 7836 5314) Reputedly London's oldest eating house, specializing in game and traditional fare

Criterion Brasserie Marco Pierre White (*224 Piccadilly, W1V 9LB* ☎ 020 7930 8380) The lavishly appointed 19C interior, reminiscent of a sultan's palace, provides a spectacular setting for fine dining.

Moderate

Cantina Vinopolis (*1 Bank End, SE1* ☎ 020 7940 8333) Located inside Vinopolis; good value.

Oxo Tower Restaurant and **Oxo Tower Brasserie** (*Barge House Street* ☎ 020 7803 3888) On the 8th floor of the Oxo Tower on the banks of the Thames. Beautiful contemporary setting enhanced by stunning views.

Fish! (*Cathedral Street, Borough Market, SE1* ☎ 020 7836 3236) Right next to Southwark Cathedral, in a large glass-enclosed market hall; very popular with fish-lovers.

Circus (*1 Upper James Street* ☎ 020 7534 4000) A fashionable restaurant-bar located in the heart of Soho.

Museum Street Cafe (*43 Museum St, WC1A 1LY* ☎ 020 7405 3211) After your visit to the British Museum, treat yourself to good food in the intimate setting of this popular Bloomsbury haunt.

People's Palace (*Royal Festival Hall, level 3* ☎ 020 7928 9999) Contemporary cuisine served in a spacious room overlooking the Thames.

Union Café (*96 Marylebone Lane, W1M 5TB* ☎ 020 7486 4860) Healthy and simple cooking is served in this casual dining room featuring an open-kitchen.

Quality Chop House (*94 Farringdon Rd , EC1R 3EA* ☎ 020 7837 5093) Traditional fare with a contemporary twist. Refectory style interior with long wooden benches and tables shared by customers.

Alfred (*245 Shaftesbury Ave, WC2H 8EH* ☎ 020 7240 2566) Innovative British fare in a contemporary stark setting. Good beers.

SHOPPING

Part of the fun of exploring London lies in discovering the city's countless small shops. Whatever you want to buy, no matter how obscure, there will almost certainly be a specialist shop devoted to it. The big stores offer a wide selection, generally at competitive prices.

A few stores are sights in themselves, worth visiting even if you have no purchases in mind – though you will surely be tempted. **Harrods**, on Brompton Road in Knightsbridge, is world-famous, glitzy and rather pricey – the tiled food halls alone repay a visit, tastefully laid out to tempt the palate. **Harvey Nichols**, on the corner of Sloane Street and Knightsbridge, specialises in fashion and furnishings. **Liberty**, on Regent Street, made its name for importing oriental fabrics, and around 1900 'Liberty style' had an enormous influence on bourgeois tastes. The store still sells lovely clothes, jewellery and fabrics. A few doors down Regent Street is **Hamleys**, the enormous toy emporium.

Main shopping areas

Covent Garden: Unusual gifts, cosmetics, food and drink, fashion. Most of the more interesting shops are in the northern half of the area, north of Long Acre and in and around Neal Street.

Soho: The eastern half, around Charing Cross Road, specializes in books, music, and food and drink. To the west, in and around Carnaby Street, look out for the menswear: **Jones** (Floral Street) and **Burro** (Newburg Street). On the same street, **Fletcher** is a boutique with its own line of clothing catering to a young market, or try **Cinch** and **Errol Peak** for casual outfits and suits, often in rather surprising fabrics. In Carnaby Street, check out the trendy wristwatches and sunglasses in **Face**.

Oxford Street and Regent Street: Department stores in Oxford Street include **John Lewis**, **Selfridges**, **Debenhams** and naturally **Marks & Spencer** (at Marble Arch and between Oxford Circus and Tottenham Court Road). Regent Street has Liberty, Hamleys, and china, cashmere and jewellery shops.

St James's: A rather rarified quarter full of fine-art dealers. Jermyn Street specializes in high-quality men's clothes and accessories. It is also a good area for wines.

Piccadilly and Bond Street: A good mixture of up-market shopping, with top-quality clothes in Burlington Arcade and Bond Street; art dealers in Cork Street (chiefly contemporary painters) and Bond Street. Jewellery can also be found on New Bond Street (notably at **Wempe**).

Knightsbridge: Alongside Harrods and Harvey Nichols, fashion boutiques mingle with antique and fine art dealers. All the big names in international fashion are on Sloane Street, from Gucci and Versace to Hermès, Dior, Armani, etc, as well as the trendiest British couture designers.

Kensington High Street: Fashion boutiques and chain stores, with antique shops along Kensington Church Street. For club- and street-wear The Kensington Fashion Fair takes place in Kensington Town Hall.

Chelsea: The King's Road mixes trendy clothes shops and treasure-troves of imaginative household accessories with chain stores.

Useful addresses

Here are a few suggestions to start you off!

Department Stores
Harrods *Knightsbridge, SW1*
Harvey Nichols *109-125 Knightsbridge, SW1*
John Lewis *278-306 Oxford Street*
Marks & Spencer *Marble Arch*
Selfridges *400 Oxford Street*

Fashion
Burberry *18-22 Haymerket, SW1* Classic trenchcoats and clothes.
Laura Ashley *256-258 Regent Street W1* Famous for its prints and designs.
Moss Bros Hire Warehouse *27 King Street, Covent Garden, WC2* Menswear for hire.
Liberty *210-220 Regent Street, W1* Another British classic.
Hyper Hyper *26-40 Kensington High Street* Offbeat designers fresh from college start here.
French Connection and **Oasis** on *King's Road* Elegant clothes at reasonable prices.
Electrum and **Butler & Wilson** *South Molton Street, W1* Jewellery.

Art and Antiques
Antiquarius *131-141 King's Road, SW3* Fashion accessories market.
Bonhams *Montpelier Street, SW7*
Christies *8-10 Kings Street, SW1*
Phillips Fine Art *101 New Bond Street, W1*
Sotheby's *34-35 New Bond Street, W1*
Spink & Son *5-7 King Street, W1* For coins and medals.

Books
Waterstones *121-125 Charing Cross Road, WC2*
Hatchards *187 Piccadilly, W1*
Foyles *113-115 Charing Cross Road, WC2*
Dillons *82 Gower Street, WC1*

Oxford Street is thronged with shoppers all year round, in search of the ultimate bargain.

Food and Drink
Fortnum & Mason *181 Piccadilly, W1*
Drury Tea and Coffee Company *37 Drury Lane, WC2*
The Tea House *15A Neal Street, WC2*
Neal's Yard Dairy *17 Shorts Garden, Covent Garden, WC2* For English cheeses.
Jeroboams *24 Bute Street, South Kensington, SW7 Cheeses.*
The Scotch House *2 Brompton Road, SW1*
The Griffin Brewery *Chiswick Lane South, W4*

Music
The three main high street chains are:
HMV *150 Oxford St, W1*
Virgin Megastore *14-30 Oxford Street, W1*
Tower Records, *Piccadilly Circus*

Specialist music shops:
Ray's Jazz Shop *180 Shaftesbury Avenue, WC2*
Black Music Centre *12 Berwick Street, W1*
58 Dean Street Records *58 Dean Street, W1*

London's Markets

It is not only tourists who head for the capital's numerous markets – but locals as well, so these are some of the best places to get a feel for contemporary life in the capital.

Just looking can be as much fun as buying. If you do feel the need to rest your legs, stop at one of the food stalls or market cafés, where you can usually find ethnic food or perhaps some old-fashioned traditional London fare, such as pie and mash or jellied eels.

Market prices generally are lower than shop prices, and there are plenty of real bargains around. Bear in mind, however, that 'you get what you pay for'. And remember that, unlike shops, stall-holders probably will not refund or exchange goods.

Bermondsey: Frequented by professional dealers as well as the public. Paintings, jewellery, silverware, Victoriana etc. *Friday 5am-1pm.*

Berwick Street: Fruit, vegetables, and cheese stalls in one of Soho's streets. Rupert Street also has clothes and leather goods, but higher prices. *Daily except Sunday, 9am-5pm.*

Brick Lane: Absolutely everything (or almost), from bicycles to jackets, antiques to electrical goods. Cosier than when it was the haunt of 'Jack the Ripper'. *Sunday 6am-1pm.*

Brixton: A lively food, clothes and general market with a strong Caribbean flavour. Good shops in Granville and Market Row Arcades. *Daily 8.30am-5.30pm except Wednesday pm and Sunday.*

Camden: Five huge, very crowded markets, popular with young people and tourists. The emphasis is on clothes, shoes and jewellery, but there are also books, antiques and crafts. Camden Lock, *Tuesday to Sunday 10am-6pm*; Camden Market, *Thursday to Sunday 9am-5.30pm*; other markets at weekends.

Camden Passage: A rather sedate market in Islington (not to be confused with Camden markets), selling prints, silverware, toys, jewellery. Attractive but pricey permanent antique shops. *Wednesday 7am-2pm; Saturday 8am-4pm; Thursday (books) 7am-4pm.*

Columbia Road: One of

Brick Lane – one of the East End's liveliest markets.

London's principal retail flower and plant markets (though the flowers are 'left-overs'), with interesting shops alongside. *Sunday 8am-12.30pm.*

Greenwich: Antiques, crafts, clothes, books, coins, bric-a-brac. The stalls in the covered market are more expensive. *Saturday and Sunday 9am-5pm.*

Petticoat Lane: Cheap new goods, such as clothes, jewellery, watches, bags and plenty of raucous backchat. *Sunday 9am-2pm.*

Piccadilly Crafts: Attractive antique and crafts (Third World) in the churchyard of St James's Piccadilly. *Thursday to Saturday 9.30am-6pm.*

Portobello Road: Thousands of stalls selling paintings, jewellery, silverware, furniture and bric-a-brac. Further on are clothes and craft stalls. Antiques *Saturday 8.30am-5.30pm;* Clothes (under Westway) *Friday 7am-4pm, Saturday 8am-5pm, Sunday 9am-4pm.*

Spitalfields: Craft, bric-a-brac and organic food stalls in the former wholesale market. Organic *Monday to Friday 9am-6pm, Sunday 11am-3pm.*

ENTERTAINMENT AND NIGHTLIFE

With literally hundreds of events every night, it is impossible to be bored in London. The weekly magazine *Time Out*, published on Wednesdays, is one of the best single source of information, with full listings of events. The *Evening Standard* newspaper (Thursday edition) also includes weekly programme guides.

Theatre

London's West End theatres have a well-earned international reputation for the range of plays and musicals on offer. The main national companies are the **National Theatre Company** (based at the Royal National Theatre on the South Bank) and the **Royal Shakespeare Company (RSC)** who play at the Barbican for part of each year. Seat prices are remarkably good value for money.

Musicals are the mainstay of the commercial theatres, which are centred in and around **Shaftesbury Avenue**. Here, many of the long-running hit musicals are always popular.

Theatres outside the West End are increasingly lively, producing some of the most challenging and exciting plays around. The **Donmar Warehouse** in Covent Garden, the **Almeida** in Islington, and **The Gate** in Notting Hill are some of the best venues.

Regent's Park offers a completely different theatrical experience. **The Open-Air Theatre** (☎ 020 7486 2431) usually stages two or three Shakespeare plays and a musical between May and September, then closes for the rest of the year. Although it only operates during the summer months, remember to take warm clothing, a cushion or blanket to sit on, an umbrella in case of rain, and a picnic.

Addresses

Barbican Arts Centre *Silk Street, EC2* ☎ 020 7638 8891 (tube: Barbican)

Her Majesty's Theatre *Haymarket, SW1* (tube: Piccadilly Circus) ☎ 020 7494 5400 For *Phantom of the Opera*.

Globe Theatre *21 New Globe Walk, Bankside* ☎ 020 7902 1400 (tube: Mansion House)

New London *167 Drury Lane, WC2* ☎ 020 7405 0072/cc bookings 7404 4079 (tube: Holborn) For Andrew Lloyd Webber's *Cats*.

Palace Theatre *Shaftesbury Avenue, W1* ☎ 020 7434 0909 (tube: Leicester Square) For *Les Misérables*.

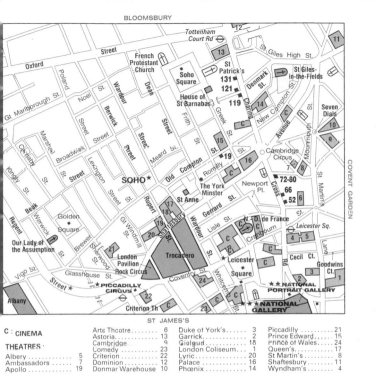

Theatre Royal Drury Lane
Catherine Street, W1 ☎ 020 7494
5000 (tube: Covent Garden)
Prince Edward Theatre *Coventry
Street, W1* ☎ 020 7447 5400
(tube: Piccadilly Circus)
Strand *Aldwych, WC2* ☎ 020
7930 8800 (tube: Charing Cross)

Music

There are three concert halls in
the **South Bank Arts Centre**.
The **Barbican**, home of the
London Symphony Orchestra,
and the **Royal Albert Hall** are
also important venues.
Wigmore Hall and St John's,
Smith Square specialise in
chamber music.

The **Royal Opera House** and
English National Opera at the
London Coliseum are the

major opera houses.

London plays host to a wide range of contemporary music and dance scenes. Nightclubs specializing in anything from house and garage, through R & B and hip-hop to the peculiarly British phenomenon of jungle/drum 'n' bass, as well as even more esoteric genres, are to be found all over the city.

Avant-garde venues such as the **Turnmills** (*63 Clerkenwell Rd*), **Fabric** (*77a Charterhouse St, EC1*), **Wag** (*33 Wardour St, W1*) and **Home** (*1 Leicester Square*) cater for London's eclectic youth. Latin-dance clubs such as **Salsa**, on Charing Cross Road, are popular, and at the mellower end of the scale, easy-listening is making a surprise comeback. Get hold of a copy of *Time Out* or *The Guest List* for details of clubs, and collect the fliers handed out round Leicester Square and other busy night-time entertainment centres.

Live music is also very popular. The **100 Club** (*100 Oxford St, W1*), **Ronnie Scott's** (*47th Frith St, Soho, W1*) and the **Jazz Café** (*5 Parkway, Camden, NW1*) are all favourites with jazz fans. Specialist venues throughout London accommodate the musical tastes of all elements of the population.

Large venues such as the **Hammersmith Apollo**, **Astoria**, **Shepherds Bush Empire** and **Brixton Academy** host concerts by major bands, and massive sell-out gigs are staged at giant venues such as **Wembley Stadium** and **London Arena**, Docklands.

Opera and Classical Music
Albert Hall *Kensington Gore, SW7* ☎ 020 7589 8212
Barbican Arts Centre *Silk Street, EC1* ☎ 020 7638 8891
London Coliseum *St Martin's Lane* ☎ 020 7632 8300
Royal Opera House *Bow Street, Covent Garden* ☎ 020 7304 4000
Wigmore Hall *36 Wigmore Street, W1* ☎ 020 7935 2141
Royal Festival Hall (Queen Elizabeth Hall, Purcell Room) *Belvedere Road, SE1* ☎ 020 7960 4242

Rock, Roots and Jazz
Academy Brixton *211 Stockwell Road, SW9* ☎ 020 7924 9999 (tube: Brixton)
Apollo Hammersmith *Queen Caroline Street, W6* ☎ 020 7416 6080 (tube: Hammersmith)
Astoria *157 Charing Cross Road, WC2* ☎ 020 7434 0403 (tube: Tottenham Court Road)
Wembley Arena *Empire Way, Wembley* ☎ 020 8900 1234 (tube: Wembley Park or Wembley Central)

Cinema

Hundreds of films are shown every day across the city. Cinemas throughout central London and the suburbs show the latest releases, but beware of the inflated prices in the West End! Smaller independent cinemas provide a wider choice, offering special-interest, foreign and 'art-house' films, as well as older mainstream ones. You can see films in 3D at the British Film Institute **IMAX Cinema** on South Bank, near Waterloo Station.

Booking

Ticket booking starts weeks, sometimes even months, in advance for popular plays, operas and concerts If you have time, go to the theatre box office – you will see exactly where you are sitting. Ticket agents charge a hefty booking fee but will save you time: **Ticketmaster** ☎ 020 7344 4444 or **First Call** ☎ 020 7420 0000 or 0870 333 7770.

The **Half-Price Ticket Booth** in Leicester Square sells a limited number of half-price theatre tickets for that day's performances only. It opens at 1pm (midday on matinée days) – queues form, so you are advised to arrive as early as you can. For more information ☎ 020 7836 0971.

SPORTS

Many health clubs and sports centres offer day membership. In central London you can **swim** at the **Oasis** (outdoor and indoor, *32 Endell Street, WC2* ☎ 020 7831 1804). For outdoor swimming try the three pools on Hampstead Heath. The Mixed Bathing Pond is in East Heath Road on the west side; the **Men's Pond** and the **Women's Pond** in Millfield Lane (☎ 020 7485 4491) are on the east side.

You can **skate** at Queen's Ice Skating Club in Queensway as well as at Broadgate (*see* p.37), go **horse riding** around Hyde Park from the Stables in Bathurst Mews (*63 Bathurst Mews, W2* ☎ 020 7723 2813), and play **tennis** in many public parks.

Popular spectator sports such as football, rugby and cricket are well catered for. The two biggest London **football** clubs are Arsenal (at Highbury) and Tottenham Hotspur (at White Hart Lane). Major cup finals and internationals are held at Wembley Stadium. International **rugby** is played at the Twickenham Rugby Football Ground.

One of the big events in June which always draws large crowds is the **Wimbledon Lawn Tennis Championships**.

THE BASICS

Before You Go

Visitors entering Britain should hold a full passport. Check that the expiry date does not occur before the end of your stay. Visas are not required for citizens of EU countries or of the US, Australia, Canada and New Zealand; travellers from other countries should check.

Pets being taken into Britain must be put into quarantine on arrival for a minimum period of six months.

Getting There

By Air: London has five airports. Heathrow, Gatwick Stansted and Luton handle international flights. London City Airport is a smaller international airport which is mainly used by commuters.

Heathrow is the largest airport, 24km (15 miles) west of central London, and has four terminals; for information ☎ **020 8759 4321**. Central London can be reached by Airbus, the underground (Piccadilly Line) or taxi. The **Heathrow Express** (30-40mins)/**Fasttrain** (15mins) link provides a fast alternative rail link into Paddington Station ☎ **0845 600 1515**. Heathrow and Gatwick are

Eurostar departing from Waterloo, bound for France via the Channel Tunnel.

linked by Speedlink, an express coach service operating 365 days a year. From Gatwick, 48km (30 miles) south of central London, fast, regular trains operate to Victoria Station and Thameslink rail services run from King's Cross and Blackfriars stations. Luton, 54km (34 miles) north of central London, is linked to St Pancras and King's Cross stations by rail and coach; buses also go to Victoria Station.

Stansted, 50km (31 miles) north-east of central London, is connected by rail to Liverpool Street and Tottenham Hale stations.

By Rail: London's mainline railway stations serving different regions of Greater London and the rest of the country are:

Charing Cross: south-east London/south-east England
Euston: west Midlands/north-west England/north Wales/Glasgow
Fenchurch Street: east London/Essex
King's Cross: north-east London/north-east England/Edinburgh/Glasgow/Aberdeen
Liverpool Street: east London/Essex/East Anglia *Paddington*: south-west England/south Midlands/south Wales
Marylebone: north-west London/south Midlands
St Pancras: north London/south and east Midlands/South Yorkshire
Victoria: south and south-east London/south and south-east England
Waterloo: south-west London/southern England/Eurostar services to France and Belgium.

For details call ☎ **0345 484 950**. Information and tickets are available at all the stations.

Channel Tunnel: Travellers from the Continent also have the option of taking the Channel Tunnel as an alternative to ferry or hovercraft.

Eurostar trains are for foot passengers only, running from Waterloo to Paris and Brussels. Some services also stop at Lille, some at Calais, and some at Ashford, Kent. Eurostar runs from about 5am-7pm ☎ **0900 186 186**.

Le Shuttle is for vehicles and their occupants only, operating between Folkestone and Calais 24 hours a day. ☎ **0990 353 535**

By Sea: If arriving by sea, there are several companies offering ferry or hovercraft crossings from France, Belgium, the Netherlands and Ireland and all the south and south-east coast ports have train and coach connections to central London.

By Coach: Coaches arrive (mostly) at Victoria Coach Station, Buckingham Palace Road SW1. For National Express Coach bookings and enquiries ☎ **0990 808080**.

By Car: If visiting London by car, parking may be a problem unless you are staying in a hotel with its own car park (rare).

A-Z

Accidents and Breakdowns

If you are in a hire car, the rental company should be able to assist you in the event of a breakdown so carry their details with you at all times.

If you are in your own car, the Automobile Association ☎ **0800 887 766** and the RAC ☎ **0800 828 282**, Britain's two main motoring organizations, offer breakdown assistance and although membership is necessary, it is possible to join on the spot (at a price).

In the event of an accident, the police should be called immediately on ☎ **999**. The ambulance and fire services can also be contacted on this number.

Accommodation see p.96

Banks

Bank opening times vary slightly, but in general they are open from Monday to Friday from 9.30am-5/5.30pm and some open on Saturdays from 9.30-12.30pm. Most have

outside cash dispensers, which accept international credit cards and are open 24 hours.

Bicycles

Cycling is a good way of getting about London, but the traffic can be hair-raising, and it is not advisable for those unused to cycling in a busy city as there are few cycle lanes. Details of cycle hire can be obtained from the London Tourist Board (see Tourist Information). Protective headgear is essential for cyclists in London, and lights and reflective bands are advisable. When not in use, bikes should always be secured to a suitable immovable object, and preferably immobilised with a D-lock or some other form of security device. Remember to check for signs before leaving your bike, as there are restrictions in some areas.

Books

Joseph Conrad *The Secret Agent*
Charles Dickens *Oliver Twist,*

Our Mutual Friend, The Old Curiosity Shop
Arthur Conan Doyle *Sherlock Holmes stories*
Doris Lessing *London Observed*
V S Pritchett *A Cab at the Door*
David Widgery *Some Lives: a GP's East End*
A N Wilson *The Sweets of Pimlico*

Camping
London is not an obvious choice for a camping or caravanning holiday, but there are a few campsites on the fringes. Camping in the city's parks is forbidden. Details of sites can be obtained from the London Tourist Board. *See* **Tourist Information Offices**

Car Hire
Car hire really only makes sense if you intend to travel out of London. All the major car-hire companies are represented in London, and cars can be hired on the spot at the airports and elsewhere. The minimum age varies from 21 to 23, but most firms charge a supplement for under 25s. A full licence, which must have been held for a year, is required. Drivers from non-English-language countries must obtain an international driving licence.

American visitors should note that hire cars usually have manual transmissions. Check in advance with the hire company to see if automatic vehicles are available.
Europcar ☎ 0870 607 5000
Avis ☎ 0870 333 8000
See also **Driving** and **Transport**

Children
Children under 16 nearly always pay a reduced entrance fee to sights and attractions, with the under fives getting in for nothing. Where there is more than one child in the party, family tickets save a bit of money. Kidsline **☎ 020 7222 8070** gives information about activities for children in and around London.

On London Transport, all children under five travel free on the underground trains and on the buses. Children from 5 to 16 years old pay a reduced fare.

Photo identity cards, issued free at Underground and main line stations, London Transport Travel Information Centres (*see* **Transport**) and Pass Agents, are required for children aged 14 and 15 to prove their age, otherwise adult fares will be charged.

Children are not welcomed quite as unreservedly in restaurants and public places as on the Continent. However, more places are catering for families

The Gryphon marks the City boundary on the Embankment.

so finding somewhere suitable to eat, stay or visit should not be too difficult. Many pubs do not allow children in, or have a separate room for families.

Climate *see* **page 94**

Clothing

Casual clothing is acceptable almost everywhere in London these days, and only the smartest restaurants insist on formal dress. It is always a good idea to have a sweater and a rainproof coat with you, however, as the unpredictability of Britain's weather – even in mid summer – is notorious. Not all buildings are fully air conditioned, and can get very stuffy in hot weather.

UK shoe sizes and women's clothes sizes differ from the US as follows:

Women's Sizes

UK	8	10	12	14	16	18
US	6	8	10	12	14	16

Men's Shoes

UK	7	7.5	8.5	9.5	10.5	11
US	8	8.5	9.5	10.5	11.5	12

Women's Shoes

UK	4.5	5	5.5	6	6.5	7
US	6	6.5	7	7.5	8	8.5

Complaints

Any complaints that cannot be satisfactorily resolved on the spot with the person in charge should be addressed, in writing, to the British Tourist Authority or the London Tourist Board (*see* **Tourist Information**).

Consulates and Embassies

Australia
Australia House,
The Strand WC2B 4LA
☎ **020 7379 4334**
Canada
Macdonald House,
1 Grosvenor Square, W1
☎ **020 7258 6600**
Ireland
17 Grosvenor Place, SW1X 7HR
☎ **020 7245 9033**
New Zealand
New Zealand House,
80 Haymarket SW1Y 4TQ

☎ **020 7930 8422**
US
24 Grosvenor Square, W1A 1AE
☎ **020 7499 9000**; for passport
matters ☎ **020 7491 3506**

Crime

There is no need to be unduly
concerned about crime in
London, but as in any big city
it is advisable to take sensible
precautions.

• Carry as little money, and
as few credit cards, as possible,
and leave any valuables in the
hotel safe.

• Carry wallets and purses in
secure pockets or wear a
money belt, and carry
handbags across your body or
firmly under your arm.

• Cars can be a target for
opportunists, so never leave
your car unlocked, and hide
away or, better still, remove
items of value.

• If you do have anything
stolen contact the nearest
police station: ☎ **192** for
Directory Enquiries.

• In an emergency contact
the police on ☎ **999**.

Customs and Entry Regulations

With the advent in 1993 of the
Single European market, tax
free allowances have increased
considerably for travellers from
EU countries and there is no
limit on the transfer of goods
for personal use. For VAT
refund *see* p.120.

Pets being taken into Britain
must be put into quarantine
on arrival as a precaution
against the spread of rabies.

Disabled Visitors

Facilities for disabled travellers
in London are improving all
the time but there are still very
many places where access is
difficult and buses and the
underground cannot easily
accommodate wheelchairs.
Check with individual hotels
and guesthouses about the
facilities they can provide.

Artsline, 54 Charlton Street,
NW1, ☎ **020 7388 2227** is a
useful telephone information
service providing advice about
theatres, cinema and gallery
access. Detailed information
about accommodation,
transport, equipment and tour
operators is published in *Access
to London*, available from
RADAR, 12 City Forum, 250
City Road, London EC1V 8AF,
☎ **020 7250 3222** between
10am and 4pm. **Tripscope**
☎ **020 8994 9294** can provide
advice about all aspects of
travel and transport for
disabled and elderly people in
Britain, and help with planning
journeys, equipment hire, etc.
London Transport (who

provide a free leaflet, *Access to the Underground*) and the **London Tourist Board** can also offer helpful information.

Driving

Even if you need a car for travelling out of London, while in the city it is far better to rely on public transport and/or taxis.

Cars drive on the left-hand side of the road and seat belts are compulsory wherever they are fitted. Speed limits are: 70mph/112kph on motorways, 60mph/96kph on main roads and generally 30mph/50kph in built-up areas. Any exceptions to these rules will be well signposted.

Parking is difficult and expensive in London and uniformed traffic wardens, who issue parking tickets imposing a fine on those infringing the regulations, are vigilant. In some places wheel clamps are put on the car, and it is a costly and time-consuming business getting them removed. Parking is permitted in pay and display zones, daytime and 24-hour car parks, or on-street where there are parking meters (the meters display the tariff; ensure you have the correct coins, and remember you cannot stay in the same space once the original time has elapsed).

It is illegal to drive while under the influence of drink, and the police can breathalyse a driver suspected of drink-driving.

Emergencies

For any emergency requiring Police, Fire or an Ambulance, ☎ **999** (free).

Etiquette

The British are a fairly orderly nation and have a strong sense of fair play; they will queue quietly for hours, for example, so impatience or ill manners do not go down well. Otherwise, there are few pitfalls that the visitor has to watch out for.

Health

Citizens of all European Union countries are entitled to free National Health Service (NHS) treatment, though there are charges for prescriptions. Citizens of other countries, however, will be charged for all medical services with the exception of emergency or accident treatment administered at NHS hospitals.

Basic medical advice and non-prescription drugs are available at chemists (pharmacies). Overseas visitors are advised to carry photocopies of their prescriptions from home.

Most are open standard shop hours (*see* **Opening Hours**) but some stay open much later. **Bliss Chemist** (*5 Marble Arch, W1* ☎ **020 7723 6116**) is open every day from 9am-midnight. **Zafash** (*233-235 Old Brompton Road, SW5* ☎ **020 7373 2798**) is open 24 hours.

Lost Property

If you lose something while travelling on public transport, contact the following numbers: London Transport buses or underground trains: ☎ **020 7222 1234** (9.30am-2pm, Monday to Friday).
British Rail trains: the main-line station where the train arrived.
Coach: Victoria Coach Station ☎ **020 7730 3466**.
Possessions left in a black taxi cab: ☎ **020 7833 0996**.
Anything lost in the street or a park should be reported to the nearest police station; ☎ **192** for Directory Enquiries.

Maps and Guidebooks

The *Michelin Green Guide London* provides detailed maps of the areas of London, and includes detailed information on the main attractions, museums, galleries and other sights. The *Michelin Red Guide London* contains details of hotels, restaurants and pubs.

For route-planning, consult Michelin on the Net: **www.michelin-travel.com**. The route planning service covers all of Europe and allows you to select your preferred route. Updated three times weekly integrating road works, detours and so on, the itineraries include distances, travel times and selected hotels and restaurants.

See also *Michelin London town plan* **no 34** (1:8 000), with one-way streets and street index.

Millennium Dome

The Dome site is car-free, apart from special car access and pre-booked parking for registered disabled visitors. There is a choice of public transport providing easy access:
Underground: North Greenwich station, on the new Jubilee Line, is just 12 minutes from Waterloo.
Boat: At peak times, boats leave piers at Waterloo (**City Cruises** ☎ **020 7740 0400**, with combined tickets for the boat and Dome entrance) and from Blackfriars every 15 minutes; and a shuttle service runs every 10 minutes between the Dome and Greenwich.
Train: From Central London or the South East to Charlton Station, where there is a transit

bus link to the Dome.
Buses: Local buses run to the North Greenwich Transport Interchange.

Money

The pound sterling (£) is divided into 100 pence (p). Coins come in denominations of 1p, 2p, 5p, 10p, 20p, 50p and £1, and a £2 coin is due to be introduced soon; notes come in denominations of £5, £10, £20 and £50. Scottish banknotes, which sometimes appear, are also legal tender.

The major credit cards are widely accepted throughout London. There is no limit to the amount of foreign currency that can be brought into or taken out of Britain.

Value Added Tax (VAT) is a sales tax which increases the cost of an item by 17.5 per cent. This is included in the price of goods, but restaurants and hotels often advertise their prices and rates without it, then add it onto the bill. Always check, therefore, whether a quoted price includes VAT. In some cases, the duty may be reclaimed by non-EU residents, and full VAT receipts should be retained.

Newspapers

The *Guardian*, *The Times*, the *Daily Telegraph*, the *Independent* and the *Financial Times* are regarded as quality dailies or broadsheets. Entertainment sections appear in the Saturday editions. The remainder of the daily papers, called the tabloids, are heavily biased towards sport and scandal.

The *London Evening Standard*, published Monday to Friday in a number of editions, the first appearing at around midday, includes listings of the main venues. On Fridays it publishes its 'Directory Supplement'.

Particularly useful to visitors are the magazines *What's On* and *Time Out* (weekly) and *Time Out – London for Visitors* (fortnightly) which list virtually everything that is going on in London.

Opening Hours

Shops are usually open from 9am-5.30/6pm, Monday to Saturday. An increasing number of shops open on Sundays, and late-night shopping (till 8pm) is common: Wednesdays in Knightsbridge, Thursdays in Oxford and Regent Streets.
Supermarkets are usually open until 8/9pm, and from 10am-4pm on Sundays. Small food shops and newsagents usually stay open until about 8pm. Several petrol stations, which

often have shops selling basic goods attached to them, are open for 24 hours.

Museums and other tourist attractions are generally open from 9/10am-6pm, Monday to Saturday, with shorter hours on Sundays and public holidays.

Pubs are legally allowed to open from 11am-11pm (except in the City), Monday to Saturday, and from noon 3pm and 7-10.30pm on Sundays, although some choose to close in the afternoons, usually from 3-6pm, on week days.

See also **Banks** and **Post Offices**

Police

In the event of any sort of trouble or emergency, including traffic accidents, the police should be called on ☎ **999**. The policemen seen

A London 'bobby'.

patrolling the streets are always willing to help with queries.

Post Offices

The main post office in London is off Trafalgar Square, at William IV Street WC2N 4DL, open Monday to Saturday 8am-8pm (Friday 8.30am-8pm). Poste restante mail should be sent here. Other London post offices are open Monday to Friday 9am-5.30pm, Saturday 9.30am-12.30/1pm.

Stamps can be bought from post offices, vending machines outside some post offices, as well as at newsagents, some shops and garages. A first class letter to anywhere in the British Isles is 26p, arrival the next day, or second class 20p, taking up to four days. Letters to EU countries also cost 36p

Public Holidays

Many shops and tourist attractions in the capital are open on public (or bank) holidays, with the exception of Christmas Day.

New Year's Day: 1 January
Good Friday (variable)
Easter Monday (variable)
First Monday in May
Last Monday in May
Last Monday in August
Christmas Day: 25 December
Boxing Day: 26 December

Trooping the Colour, one of London's royal ceremonies.

If 1 January, 25 December or 26 December fall on a Saturday or Sunday, the following weekday is taken as a public holiday.

Religion

London is a multi-cultural city, and there are churches representing all faiths in the city. Consult London's Yellow Pages under 'Places of Worship'.

Sightseeing

Numerous companies offer tours of the city, but taking a sightseeing tour on an open-topped double-decker bus is one of the best ways of seeing the sights. Most have live com-mentaries in English and some have recorded commentaries in other languages. Departure points are located all over the city, and many services are the hop-on, hop-off variety. Details of all the possible options are available from the London Tourist Board. Among these is the **Original London Sightseeing Tour** ☎ **020 8877 1722** or, if you want to plan your tour in advance, www.theoriginaltour.com (*see* **Tourist Information**).

Joining a guided walk is another good way of getting to know London. Details of these tours can be obtained from the London Tourist Board or from

Time Out or *What's On*
(*see* **Newspapers**).

For those who fancy a river trip, there are regular cruises along the Thames, plus special lunch and evening cruises. Boats for private hire are also available. For information call London Tourist Board River Trips on ☎ **0839 123 432.** Another option is a trip on the Regent's Canal from Little Venice or Camden Lock canal basins. Call ☎ **020 7482 2660** for information.

Smoking
Smoking is not tolerated as widely as it used to be in London. It is banned in most public buildings and offices and on all public transport. Some hotels and restaurants are totally non-smoking establishments. Most cafés and restaurants are divided into non-smoking and smoking areas.

Telephones
Public payphones are found all over the city. Most now accept coins (10p, 20p, 50p £1), phonecards and credit and charge cards. Phonecards can be bought from post offices, newsagents, some supermarkets and petrol stations. They come in denominations of £2, £5, £10 and £20. As elsewhere, telephoning from your hotel

room can be expensive.

International calls, as well as calls to any other part of Britain, are cheapest between 6pm and 8am and all day Saturday and Sunday.

To dial out of England, ☎ **00** followed by the country code, the area code (without the 0 if there is one) and subscriber number.
Country codes are as follows:
Australia: **61**
Canada: **1**
Ireland: **353**
New Zealand: **64**
USA: **1**
Useful numbers:
UK operator ☎ **100**
International operator ☎ **155**
UK directory enquiries ☎ **192**
Overseas directory enquiries ☎ **153**
Talking Pages (a very useful information service) is on ☎ **0800 600 900.**
020 is the code for London, followed by an 8-digit number, beginning with **7** for inner London or **8** for outer London. If you are calling from within London, this code does not have to be dialled.

Numbers beginning **0891, 0660, 0839, 0881, 0991, 0632, 0541, 0331, 0336, 0338** and **0836** are all charged at premium (higher) rate.

Any number beginning **0800** is free.

Time Difference

Greenwich Mean Time (GMT) is used from late October to late March. In March the clocks go forward one hour for British Summer Time (BST), and in October they go back an hour to accord with GMT.

Tipping

Check whether or not a service charge has already been included in café, restaurant and hotel bills; if not, a tip of 10 per cent is normal. Taxi drivers and hairdressers expect a similar tip. It is usual to give cloakroom attendants and porters up to 50p.

Toilets

Public toilets are few and far between in London, and those that do exist tend to be poorly maintained. Any establishment serving alcohol is obliged to have toilets, and all public buildings have them. Publicans and restaurant owners do not take kindly to people walking in off the street solely to use their facilities. Department stores are a good alternative. Toilets at main-line stations are usually of a reasonable standard.

Tourist Information Offices

The **London Tourist Board**, 26 Grosvenor Gardens SW1, ☎ 020 7730 3488 operates several tourist information centres in London. The main offices are at Victoria Station Forecourt, Heathrow Information Centre, Liverpool Street Underground Station and the basement of Selfridges, in Oxford Street. The **Britain Visitor Centre** is at 1 Lower Regent Street, SW1Y 4NS.

Other tourist information centres include:

British Travel Centre, 12 Regent Street SW1Y 4PQ (no telephone enquiries)

City of London Information Centre, St Paul's Churchyard EC4M 8BX ☎ 020 7332 1456/7

Docklands Visitor Centre, 3 Limeharbour, Isle of Dogs E14 9TJ ☎ 020 7512 1111

Greenwich Tourist Information Centre, 46 Greenwich Church Street SE10 9BL ☎ 020 8858 6376

Richmond Tourist Information Centre, Old Town Hall, Whittaker Avenue, Richmond TW9 1TP ☎ 020 8940 9125

Twickenham Information Centre, The Atrium, Civic Centre, York Street, Twickenham Middx TW1 3BZ ☎ 020 8891 7272.

British Tourist Authority offices abroad are as follows:

Australia 210 Clarence Street, 8th Floor, Sydney, NSW 2000 ☎ 612 267 4666

Traditional red phone boxes.

Canada 111 Avenue Road, Suite 450, Toronto, Ontario M5R 3J8 ☎ **416 961 8124**
Ireland BTA, 18-19 College Green, Dublin 2
☎ **1 670 8000**
New Zealand BTA, Suite 305 3rd Floor, Dilworth Building, Queens Street, Auckland
☎ **(649) 303 1446**
US 2580 Cumberland Parkway, Suite 470, Atlanta, GA
☎ **(404) 432 9641**;
625 North Michigan Avenue, Suite 1510, Chicago, IL 60611
☎ **312 787 0490**; World Trade Centre, Suite 450, 350 South Figueroa Street, Los Angeles, CA 90071 ☎ **(213) 628 3525**;
551 Fifth Avenue, Suite 701, New York, NY 10176
☎ **(212) 986 2266**.

Transport

Public transport is very good in London, consisting of Underground (tube) trains and buses, both run by London Transport.

The **Underground** network consists of 12 colour-coded lines, one of which denotes the Docklands Light Railway (DLR) on which underground tickets are also valid. Nearly 300 stations are linked by the network and it is a good idea to obtain a tube map at the outset to help you find your way around. Tickets are available from a ticket office or ticket machine at all underground stations. Six fare zones are in operation and the price of your ticket depends on how many zones you travel through. Single tickets and returns are suitable if you only plan to make one tube journey, but if you plan to travel around it is a good idea to purchase a One Day or Weekend Travelcard, which will also be accepted on buses and trains within your chosen zones. It is also possible to buy weekly, monthly or even annual Travelcards, but to obtain one of these you will first need a photocard, so take along a passport-sized photograph. Many stations now have automatic ticket gates; remember to retrieve your

The London Transport sign.

ticket as you walk through. Underground trains stop running at about 12.30am.

London's red **buses** (some are painted different colours) are famous and their routes cover the entire city. On some, you pay the driver (or show your pass) on entry; others have conductors. Night buses operate through the night.

For information about London Transport visit one of their Travel Information Centres located at Euston and Victoria railway stations, King's Cross, Liverpool Street, Oxford Circus, Piccadilly Circus, St James's Park Underground stations and at Heathrow Airport and Hammersmith and West Croydon bus stations. For 24-hour information call **London Transport Travel**

Information ☎ 020 7222 1234.

Traditional black (some other colours are also seen) London **taxis** are available at airports, railway stations, and cab ranks, and cruise the streets night and day (special rates apply after midnight). All are metered and the driver is obliged to take the shortest possible route. They are available when the yellow light is on.

Several **coach** companies operate reasonably priced services to all parts of the British Isles.

TV and Radio

There are five main television channels in Britain: BBC1, BBC 2, ITV, Channel 4, and Channel 5. Some hotels have satellite and cable television with a wide range of channels showing films, sport, news and some overseas programmes.

The BBC radio stations range from current chart hits (Radio 1 and 2) to classical music (Radio 3). Radio 4 combines current affairs, arts and drama, while Radio 5 Live concentrates on sport and news. The World Service offers diverse programmes 24 hours a day. Local commercial stations cover specific styles of music, chat or rolling news.

INDEX

INDEX